FATIMA

PAUL SENZ

Fatima

*100 Questions and Answers
about the Marian Apparitions*

IGNATIUS PRESS   SAN FRANCISCO

Cover art
Crowd Looking at the Miracle of the Sun
Illustração Portugueza (October 29, 1917)
Esemono, Wikimedia Commons

Cover design by Enrique J. Aguilar

© 2020 by Ignatius Press, San Francisco
All rights reserved
ISBN 978-1-62164-437-8 (PB)
ISBN 978-1-64229-133-9 (eBook)
Library of Congress Control Number 2020938955
Printed in the United States of America ∞

To my wife, Chantel, and our children, Sidda, Doura, Ira, and Genny. Thank you for your support, your patience, and your encouragement as I wrote this—hopefully the first book of many. Thank God for you, and God bless you.

And to Our Blessed Mother, whom I have loved so dearly since before I can remember. Ora pro nobis, sancta Dei Genetrix.

CONTENTS

The October Apparition and the Miracle
of the Sun

The Popes and Our Lady of Fatima

Canonizing the Visionaries

The Assassination Attempt on John Paul II

Christian Devotion to Mary

FOREWORD

by Edward Sri

Imagine a pope approaching a statue of Mary while carrying a most unusual item in his hand: not flowers, not a rosary, not a religious medal, but, of all things, a bullet. As he draws near, the supreme pontiff of the Catholic Church places the bullet in the crown on Mary's head and repeatedly says to her, "You saved me, you saved me, you saved me ..."

That's what happened on May 13, 1982, when Pope Saint John Paul II visited the apparition site of Our Lady of Fatima in Portugal, exactly one year after he had been shot in Saint Peter's Square. In his prayer at Fatima, John Paul wasn't just giving thanks to Mary in a general way. He was recognizing the crucial role the apparitions of Our Lady of Fatima had in summing up the drama of the last century—a drama in which John Paul himself had been caught up in a most profound way.

The six apparitions of Mary to three children in Fatima, Portugal, in the year 1917 are celebrated, in part, for the many predictions that came true over the course of the twentieth century. Our Lady foretold the end of the First World War and the rise of another, more devastating global war if people did not repent. She also predicted the rise of Communist Russia, which would provoke more wars, famine, and persecutions of the Church. Her most intriguing prediction, perhaps, came in the mysterious so-called "Third Secret" of Fatima. During the apparition on July 13, 1917, the children received three dramatic visions, culminating with an image of tremendous devastation and a "bishop in white"—whom the children took to be a pope—being killed alongside other martyrs.

Pope Saint John Paul II eventually came to see this last vision as pointing to himself when on May 13, 1981, he was shot in Saint Peter's Square in an assassination attempt that nearly took his life. Two bullets hit his abdomen, but neither struck a vital organ. One bullet came only inches away from piercing his heart and aorta. The date of the attack was the anniversary of the first apparition of Mary at Fatima: May 13. Reflecting on the vision of the Third Secret, John Paul II concluded that it was Our Lady of Fatima who protected him. He later said that while the assassin's hand fired the shot, "it was a mother's hand that guided the bullet's path and in his throes the Pope halted at the threshold of death."[1]

John Paul II's strong devotion to Our Lady of Fatima focused on one particular request she made. In fact, it was the only request she made in any of her six apparitions. She asked people to pray the Rosary daily. In a world turning away from God, from the family, and

---

[1] Quoted in Congregation for the Doctrine of the Faith, *The Message of Fatima* (June 26, 2000).

from peace, and with the rise of Communist Russia and another great world war on the horizon, Mary, more than one hundred years ago in Fatima, called on the faithful to turn to the Rosary. In more recent memory, Saint John Paul II called us to do the same.

While the atheistic regimes of the twentieth-century Soviet empire have collapsed, new forms of oppression are rampant today—the "dictatorship of relativism", for example, which punishes anyone who proclaims moral truth; the "throwaway culture" or "culture of death", which views weak, innocent human persons such as the unborn, the handicapped, the poor, and the elderly not as persons to be loved, but as burdens to be avoided at all costs or even disposed of; the breakdown of marriage and family, not only in practice but even in our very definition of these sacred realities.

Near the start of the twentieth century, Mary exhorted the faithful to turn to the Rosary in order to face the great trials of that generation. Though the challenges today may be different, they are no less dramatic and arguably much more severe. If we want to build strong marriages, protect our families, and secure peace in the world, let's remember Our Lady of Fatima and turn to the power of the Rosary.

Mary challenged us to pray the Rosary not just every once in a while, when it's convenient or when we feel like it. She called us to be faithful in praying it *daily*. So one important way we can live the message of Fatima today is to honor Our Lady and incorporate the Rosary into our daily lives. This is something within our reach. Though the Rosary is sometimes viewed as a marathon devotion, we do not have to pray it all at once. We can say a few decades in the car on the way to work, another decade or two while folding laundry or doing the dishes, and one more before going to bed at night. Even if we have never prayed the Rosary consistently or have fallen away from the practice, we can start now. We don't have to be experts in praying the Rosary to get a lot out of it. As I've written elsewhere,

> Think of the rosary as being like the ocean: There's something in it for everyone, whether you consider yourself a veteran mystic longing to go deeper in prayer with our Lord, a novice struggling to learn how to pray, or someone seeking the Lord's help, right now, with something going on in your life. The deep-sea explorer and the child making sand castles on the beach can fully enjoy the same ocean while playing at different levels. And this is true with the rosary.[2]

So whatever level of Rosary praying we may think we are at, one simple way we can begin to live the message of Fatima today is by starting (or renewing) our commitment to this devotion. And let's do so with confidence that our prayers really do make a difference in the world. When we pray, our lives change, situations change, even the world can change. We can see this important truth when considering how the mystery of Fatima's Third Secret unfolded in history. With millions of people around the world heeding the message

---

[2] Edward Sri, *Praying the Rosary Like Never Before: Encounter the Wonder of Heaven and Earth* (Cincinnati: Servant, 2017), p. 2.

of Our Lady of Fatima to repent and pray—the Rosary in particular—the world became a different place than it would have been had people not responded to her call. According to Joseph Ratzinger, that was indeed the case with what happened to John Paul II on the day of his attempted assassination. In his theological explanation of the visions of Fatima, Ratzinger stated: "That here 'a mother's hand' had deflected the fateful bullet only shows once more that there is no immutable destiny, that faith and prayer are forces which can influence history and that in the end prayer is more powerful than bullets and faith more powerful than armies."[3]

To appreciate better the message of Fatima, Paul Senz has written this clear, concise guide, *Fatima: 100 Questions and Answers about the Marian Apparitions*. This is a much-needed resource that unpacks the history, message, and meaning of Our Lady of Fatima for people today. This easy-to-read, well-researched book makes it simple for readers to be introduced quickly to Our Lady of Fatima and understand her significance for our times. The question and answer format takes us on a journey through the historical background and meaning of the dramatic events associated with these apparitions. What do we know about the children of Fatima? Why would Mary appear to them? What were the so-called "Secrets of Fatima", and what is their theological meaning? What really happened with the "Miracle of the Sun" during Mary's last appearance there? And how can we live the message of Fatima today?

[3] Congregation for the Doctrine of the Faith, *The Message of Fatima*.

Paul Senz has done the Church a great service by writing this book, and it's a timely one in 2020, as this work can accompany the feature film *Fatima* being released this year. If you desire to know more about Our Lady of Fatima and share her message with others, this book is a must-read.

Dr. Edward Sri
Author, *Praying the Rosary Like Never Before*
Pentecost Sunday, 2020

PREFACE

In 1917, three young shepherd children were blessed with a series of visitations from the Blessed Virgin Mary. From May to October 1917, Lucia dos Santos, Francisco Marto, and Jacinta Marto saw her six times. During these apparitions, they received instructions from Our Lady, saw visions (including some prophetic), and witnessed miraculous healings and a cosmic miracle in which the sun appeared to dance in the sky. At first, the children did not know who was appearing to them; she told them she was from heaven, so they would refer to her as "the Lady" or "the beautiful lady from heaven".

The site of these apparitions has become one of the most important sites of pilgrimage in the world, and Our Lady of Fatima one of the most recognizable and well-known titles of Mary.

Multiple feature films have been made dramatizing the events at Fatima, including *The Miracle of Our Lady of Fatima* (1952), *The 13th Day* (2009), and *Fatima* (2020), among others. These films are artistic representations of what happened, not meant to be slavishly historically accurate in every detail. The filmmakers take a certain amount of legitimate creative license. For those who read this book in tandem with viewing one of these films, this book will serve as a companion, a guide, giving more factual context and answering your questions about the real apparitions of Our Lady of Fatima.

BACKGROUND

1. Where is Fatima? What was it like there in 1917?

Fatima is a town in Portugal, about a hundred miles north of Lisbon, the nation's capital. In 1917, Fatima was a small village. The heart of the town was the parish church, Saint Anthony, where the three Fatima visionaries—Lucia, Francisco, and Jacinta—were baptized, and where Lucia received her First Holy Communion. The townspeople were by and large Catholic, and ardently so, which meant that the church was one of the most important buildings in town.

Clusters of small homes, called hamlets, surrounded the church. One of these hamlets was known as Aljustrel, and this is where the families of the visionaries lived. Another nearby hamlet, Valinhos, would become the site of one of the apparitions. The three children often grazed their sheep in the Cova da Iria, a small pasture more than a mile outside Aljustrel, owned by Lucia's parents. This is where the other five apparitions occurred.

The people of Fatima were mostly farmers, peasants who worked hard to earn a living. They were devout, with a profound yet simple faith. This faith was unshakable, and for many this steadfastness even led to skepticism when it came to the possibility of apparitions in their own town. To them, the tenets and subjects of the faith were so profound, so transcendent, that they could not fathom something like a vision of the Blessed Virgin Mary taking place in their own village. That sort of thing may happen in Lourdes and Tepeyac, but not in Fatima. So they thought.

2. When did Christianity come to Portugal?

Portugal's position on the European continent made it well suited to receive the Christian faith at a very early date. To the north and east is Spain, to the south and west the Atlantic Ocean. This large coastline on the southwestern extreme of Europe has made Portugal an important player in maritime history, with a powerful navy and many successful explorers, giving access to Europe from other parts of the world via the ocean.

It appears that Christianity arrived in Portugal during the first century A.D., brought—legend has it—by the apostle Saint James, who traveled over the Iberian Peninsula preaching the gospel. This seems to be when the seeds of Christianity were planted, and they quickly yielded great fruit.

3. Where did the name Fatima come from?

After the Muslim Moors were defeated and fled the country in the mid-twelfth century, a Christian knight named Don Gonçalo Hermingues captured a Muslim princess named Fatima, after Muhammad's eldest daughter. They fell in love, and she converted to the Catholic faith before they were married. At her conversion, she was baptized under the name Oureana—the namesake of Ourem, a larger town near Fatima, which also lends its name to the whole administrative district where Fatima is located. She died within a year of their marriage, and Gonçalo became a Cistercian monk. When he was sent to a small priory, he took with him the remains of his wife and named the place Fatima in her honor.

4. Do the Portuguese have a particular devotion to Mary?

Yes, they do. There are several historical anecdotes that illustrate the Portuguese devotion to Mary.

In the eighth century, Muslim Moors invaded and took control of the Iberian Peninsula (modern-day Spain and Portugal). A few hundred years later, in 1139, the Portuguese once again won their independence by defeating the Moors decisively. The first king of Portugal was King Afonso I, who credited their victory over the Moors to the intercession of the Blessed Virgin Mary. To commemorate this triumph, he built the stunningly beautiful Cistercian monastery and church of Santa Maria de Alcobaça.

In the fourteenth century, the Portuguese were trying to defend themselves from a takeover by Spain. They were severely outnumbered, and it did not look like they had much of a chance of defeating Spain's superior forces. Saint Nuno Álvares Pereira led them in battle, and they turned specifically to Our Lady for her intercession. On August 14, 1385, Spain was defeated and repelled by the Portuguese forces. King John I built the magnificent Dominican monastery of Saint Mary of Victory in the Battle, known simply as Batalha—"battle".

Portugal has been referred to as the "Land of Holy Mary" from its earliest days. Since 1646, the time of King John IV, Mary has been proclaimed the queen and patroness of Portugal. In fact, the Portuguese kings traditionally did not wear crowns, because this was exclusively the right of the Mother of God as queen.

5. What is an apparition?

An apparition is a supernatural vision of sorts, where the seer (the person who claims to have had such a vision) sees something appear to him in his own surroundings. As opposed to a vision—which often brings the person out of himself, watching something as if removed from the scene—an apparition happens "here and now" and is even evident to the senses, although many apparitions are perceived by the seers alone.

If deemed necessary, the proper Church authorities will investigate claims of an apparition and make a judgment as to whether or not the apparition is "worthy of belief" (see questions 80–85).

6. What was going on in Europe when the Fatima apparitions began?

At that time, Europe, and indeed the entire world, was embroiled in the most devastating and (up to that time) deadliest conflict the world had ever seen. In July 1914, the continent was plunged into a war that caused such destruction and so disrupted the lives of millions that it became known as the Great War, or the War to End All Wars—later, the First World War. Nations throughout Europe, and eventually all over the world, were pulled into the conflict that was sparked by the assassination of Franz Ferdinand, the archduke and heir to the throne of the Austro-Hungarian Empire. Portugal did not enter the war at first, remaining officially neutral, although its treaty alliances aligned it with Great Britain. However, in March 1916, Germany declared war on Portugal, and despite the country's small size and population, many Portuguese soldiers joined the war effort. Thousands of young men across the nation were called up to fight in this conflict.

This was the deadliest war the world had ever seen, resulting in the deaths of around twenty million people worldwide. The pope called it "the suicide of civilized Europe".

7. What role did the Church play in the First World War?

The pope during this time was Benedict XV. He maintained a strictly neutral stance, so that he could operate as a mediator, a peacemaker. He worked tirelessly, making offers at every turn to help negotiate an accord, to advise the warring countries on a peaceful resolution. To his great frustration and disappointment, he was consistently turned down. Not only were these nations not interested in negotiating peace, but the pope no longer had the temporal or pastoral authority once bound up with the office.

The pope did what he could, including assisting civilians who faced deportation or who lived in areas ravaged by the conflict, and he negotiated prisoner-of-war exchanges, among other things.

There is one more thing the pope could do: he could pray and ask the world's Catholics to pray with him. Since his terrestrial attempts at brokering peace appeared to be futile, Benedict emphasized more and more prayer to end the conflict. On May 5, 1917, he began a novena to the Queen of Peace and encouraged Catholics all over the world to pray it with him. The Queen answered the earnest prayers of the Holy Father just eight days later, in Fatima.

8. Was Catholicism still important and influential in Portugal in 1917?

In 1917, Portugal was engulfed by an anti-Catholic persecution. Revolutionary forces had assassinated the king in 1908, fueled by the same ideology as the regicidal Jacobins in the French Revolution more than a century earlier: anti-monarchy, anti-Catholic, and anti-clerical. The government of the new republic immediately engaged in a program of persecution of the Church. Most religious orders were disbanded; prominent or influential clergy were either jailed or exiled from the country; Church property was confiscated by the government; and those priests who were allowed to stay in the country were given strict guidelines as to what they could and could not preach about, as well as being banned from wearing clerical garb in public. The government was attempting to quash all power, influence, and public presence of the Catholic Church.

On April 20, 1911—just six years before the apparitions began—Portugal passed the Law of Separation of Church and State. The leader of the nation's Freemasons, who had taken hold of the country, bragged that this law and other anti-Catholic measures would result in the elimination of Catholicism in Portugal within two generations.

It is important to note that, while the government may have been engaged in a campaign to make the Church disappear, rural areas remained staunchly Catholic, and individuals there were much less likely to join in this anti-Catholic movement. In fact, the rapidity with which the story of the Fatima apparitions initially spread was due to the fervor of people in the countryside, who sincerely hoped that the apparitions were God's intervention to quell the government's persecution of the Church.

THE VISIONARIES

9. Who witnessed the apparitions at Fatima? Who were the visionaries?

There were three visionaries who experienced the apparitions of Our Lady of Fatima: Lucia dos Santos, Francisco Marto, and Jacinta Marto. Francisco and Jacinta were brother and sister, and they were cousins of Lucia. When Our Lady first appeared to the children on May 13, 1917, Lucia was ten years old, Francisco nine, and Jacinta just seven.

10. Who was Lucia dos Santos?

Lucia dos Santos was born on March 28, 1907, in the hamlet of Aljustrel in Fatima. (For legal purposes, her birthday was registered as March 22.) She was the youngest of the seven children of Antonio dos Santos and Maria Rosa. Lucia had one brother and five sisters, one of whom died in infancy. Lucia's father was a farmer. The family was somewhat poor, but they owned a good deal of land, including the Cova da Iria pasture.

Lucia's mother was very religious, even devout; her father was relatively indifferent to the faith. But they both lived the Catholic faith and saw it as their responsibility to help the poor and sick as much as they could.

They observed Church feasts, followed the laws of the Church, and passed all of this along to their children. Maria Rosa also taught catechism classes at the Church of Saint Anthony in addition to her duties at home. The family would recite the Rosary together regularly.

Lucia's personality was one of joy and liveliness. This was attractive to the other boys and girls of the village, who would follow her around and even bring their own flocks along to graze where she brought hers.

Lucia was passionate about her faith from a very early age. Her mother taught her the teachings of the Church, and by the time Lucia was six years old, her mother thought she was ready to receive her First Holy Communion. Since her older sister was preparing to receive the sacraments, Lucia's mother sent her along as well to prepare. On the day before she was set to receive her First Communion, the priest said Lucia would need to wait until the following year. The young girl pleaded, and a visiting priest took pity, brought her aside, and questioned her about the faith. This visiting priest determined that Lucia was ready, even at such a young age, so she did receive the Eucharist. Lucia said that after this, she lost all interest in things of the world and only felt at home when she could be in solitude and reflect upon her First Communion.

11. Who was Francisco Marto?

Francisco Marto was born on June 11, 1908, in the hamlet of Aljustrel in Fatima. The son of Manuel Pedro

"Ti" Marto and Olimpia de Jesus, Francisco was the second youngest of their eleven children, brother of Jacinta Marto, and cousin to Lucia dos Santos. In her memoirs, Lucia described Francisco as naturally quiet and submissive; he was the sort who did not like to make requests, did not like to express his preferences, and would rather yield to others. He did not like competition, so he always lost games. Even if someone took something that belonged to him, Francisco did not care; this did not strike him as an injustice that needed to be rectified, and he simply let him have it.

Francisco loved the simple things in life. He was fascinated by nature and loved animals: lizards, snakes, and especially birds. Once, he gave a friend a penny—all the money he had—to purchase a bird the friend had captured, only to turn around and set it free. He was musically gifted, as well. His favorite activity was to go to the mountains, to the highest point he could find, sit on top of the highest rock he could climb, and make music. Sometimes he would sing, sometimes he would play his flute. His sister, Jacinta, loved to dance and loved when he would play the flute.

Francisco was moved greatly by the apparitions of Our Lady. He hated the fact that our sins are so offensive to God and cause so much sorrow for Our Lady. He grew to love any suffering he was given throughout his life, because it gave him an opportunity to offer his pain to God in reparation for the many sins committed by the world and for the conversion of sinners. Francisco desired profoundly to receive his First Holy

Communion, but by the time the visions started, he still had not.

12. Who was Jacinta Marto?

Jacinta Marto was born on March 11, 1910, the youngest of the children of Ti Marto and Olimpia de Jesus. She was the sister of Francisco Marto and cousin of Lucia dos Santos.

Of the three visionaries, Jacinta was the youngest; at the same time, she had probably the strongest resolve, the greatest determination. She could be extremely stubborn at times, with a very sensitive temperament. She was possessive and assertive; when it came to playing games, Jacinta insisted on choosing the games and partners. If the other children argued or opposed her plans, she would pout and insist.

When she wanted to be, Jacinta could certainly be sweet, kind, and gentle. She had a personality that attracted people to her, and she was deeply loved. Jacinta loved to play, dance, and sing; she also, like her brother, had a deep love for nature, because it brought to mind God and the wonders of his creation. She would be moved to tears when hearing about or meditating on the Passion of Jesus, and she longed to receive Our Lord in Holy Communion.

Like her brother and cousin, Jacinta was wise beyond her years. She had an impressive grasp of the horror of sin and a deep desire for everyone to go to heaven.

13. Why would God choose children as the visionaries at Fatima?

It seems that one of the reasons God chose children to be the visionaries at Fatima is that Portugal found itself at that moment in a very sorry state, guided in large part by Freemasons, anti-Catholics, and other so-called sophisticates in power. Children were perhaps the most likely to stand out, to serve as a metaphorical splash of cold water in the faces of the secular elite. As Saint Paul wrote to the Corinthians, "God chose what is foolish in the world to shame the wise, God chose what is weak in the world to shame the strong" (1 Cor 1:27). It is precisely because of their innocence, their simple yet profound faith, that the children were such effective messengers.

THE ANGEL OF PEACE

14. Did the children witness any other apparitions before the Lady came in May 1917?

Yes. In the spring and summer of 1916, the children were visited by the "Angel of Peace" three times. The angel did not explicitly mention the subsequent apparitions of Our Lady, but he did set the stage and prepare their hearts to hear what Our Lady had to say. He taught them that peace would be reached through prayer, sacrifice, and suffering and that the children themselves would need to experience a great deal of suffering, make many sacrifices, and pray a great deal before they could expect it of others.

15. What happened during the apparitions of the Angel of Peace?

In her memoirs, Lucia could not recall the exact dates of these apparitions, so she estimated when they occurred. In the spring of 1916, Lucia, Francisco, and Jacinta were tending their sheep at a favorite grazing spot called the Cabeco. After lunch, they prayed their daily Rosary. It is interesting to note that the children always prayed their Rosary, though with their own modifications. In order to get to play as quickly as possible, they would often say simply the first two words of the prayers on each bead—"Our Father, Hail Mary, Hail Mary, Hail Mary ..."

After finishing their abbreviated Rosary, they began to play, when suddenly a strong wind blew through, and the children saw a young man, whiter than snow, very beautiful. He said to them: "Do not be afraid. I am the Angel of Peace. Pray with me." The angel then knelt down and bowed his head until his forehead touched the ground; the children followed his example. He then taught them a prayer, which later came to be known as the Pardon Prayer: "My God, I believe, I adore, I hope, and I love you! I ask pardon of you for those who do not believe, do not adore, do not hope, and do not love you." The angel repeated this prayer three times, then stood up and said: "Pray in this way. The hearts of Jesus and Mary are attentive to the voice of your supplications." Then he vanished.

The children were overcome with a sense of the presence of God, and they stayed in the prone position praying fervently, hardly aware of how much time passed. After it was over, they did not even speak among themselves about the apparition. Lucia would later say that the appearances of the angel brought upon them an overwhelming feeling that made them practically unable to speak.

In the summer of 1916, at a well near the Santos family home, the angel appeared to the children again. He asked them what they were doing and said: "Pray! Pray very much! The hearts of Jesus and Mary have designs of mercy on you. Offer prayers and sacrifices constantly to the Most High." He told them to make a sacrifice at every opportunity, offering it as reparation for the sins that offend God and for the conversion of sinners. He called himself the Angel of Portugal, the guardian of the country. He then told them that they would suffer and that they should accept and bear these sufferings. The young children learned a great lesson from this apparition: the importance, value, and efficacy of sacrifice and suffering. This would prove to be an important preparation for the words Our Lady would speak to them.

The angel appeared a third time in late September or early October of 1916. The children were grazing the sheep at the Cabeco again, praying the Pardon Prayer repeatedly with their heads to the ground. A tremendous light shone around them, and the angel appeared, holding a chalice in his left hand with a eucharistic Host over it. The Host was dripping blood, which fell into the chalice. The angel knelt with the children, bowing his head, and the chalice and Host remained suspended in the air. Together, the four adored Jesus in the Blessed Sacrament.

The angel taught another prayer to the children: "Most Holy Trinity, Father, Son and Holy Spirit, I adore you profoundly, and I offer you the most precious Body, Blood, Soul, and Divinity of Jesus Christ, present in all the tabernacles of the world, in reparation for the outrages, sacrileges and indifference with which he himself is offended. And through the infinite merits of his most Sacred Heart, and the Immaculate Heart of Mary, I beg of you the conversion of poor sinners."

Now comes the most extraordinary part of the angel's appearances to the children. At this point, Lucia was the only one of these children who had received First Communion. The angel stood, took the chalice and Host into his hands, and gave the Host to Lucia; he then gave the chalice to Francisco and Jacinta to drink. This, then, was Francisco and Jacinta's First Holy Communion. The angel said to them all: "Take and drink the Body and Blood of Jesus Christ, horribly outraged by ungrateful men. Make reparation for their crimes and console your God." Then, after praying with his head bowed to the ground, he departed.

16. Did the Angel of Peace tell the children they would be having more visions?

No. His apparitions had their own message of prayer and sacrifice, of accepting with joy the suffering that God brings you and doing all of this in reparation for the sins that have offended God and for the conversion of sinners. These themes would carry through the apparitions of Our Lady several months later.

THE MAY APPARITION

*17. What happened during the first apparition
of Our Lady at Fatima?*

May 13, 1917, was a Sunday. Lucia dos Santos, Francisco
Marto, and Jacinta Marto went to early Mass and then
took their flocks of sheep to the Cova da Iria ("Cove of
Irene" or "Cove of Peace"). While the sheep grazed in
the field, the children ate lunch and then prayed.

It was a sunny day, with a clear blue sky—but the children saw what seemed like a flash of lightning. Thinking that a thunderstorm was coming, they started to rush
home, when they saw another flash. Then, suddenly,
there was a woman dressed in white on top of a small
holm oak tree. She radiated a brilliant, dazzling light; her
clothes seemed almost to be made of light. She looked to
the children to be around seventeen years old. There was
a cord around her neck with a ball of light hanging from
it; toward the bottom of her tunic there was a star, and
she held a rosary that gave off a celestial shine.

The woman spoke and said, "Do not be afraid. I
will do you no harm." The children immediately felt at
ease in her presence. They were filled with joy. At first,
Francisco could not see the Lady and wondered who his
cousin was talking to. After a short while, he could see

her, but was never able to hear her. Jacinta could see her and hear her, but could not speak to her. Lucia could see and hear her and was able to speak with her.

Lucia asked, "Where are you from?" The Lady answered, "I am from heaven." Lucia then asked what the Lady wanted of her, to which she responded that she wanted the children to return on the thirteenth of every month for six months, at that same hour. She said that she would tell them at a later time who she was and what she wanted.

Since the woman came from heaven and the children felt so deeply that they could trust her, Lucia asked if they too would go to heaven. The Lady told them that they would, but Francisco would need to say many rosaries first.

The Lady then asked the children an important question—one that would set the tone for the rest of the apparitions, and indeed for the rest of their lives: "Are you willing to offer yourselves to God and bear all the sufferings He wills to send you, as an act of reparation for the sins by which He is offended and of supplication for the conversion of sinners?" The children responded joyfully that, yes, they were willing. She told them they would suffer a great deal, but their comfort would be the grace of God.

She opened her hands, and a great light enveloped the children. An impulse moved the children to drop to their knees and pray: "O most Holy Trinity, I adore you! My God, my God, I love you in the most Blessed Sacrament!" Then the Lady told them to pray the Rosary every day for peace in the world and for an end to the war. She rose and disappeared in the east.

Lucia begged her cousins not to tell anyone about the visions, and they all agreed.

18. Mary said we need to pray for world peace. Why are our prayers needed? Why wouldn't God just grant peace to the world?

Certainly, God is all-powerful. But he gave his people free will, and he desires that we use our free will for good. Saint Augustine said it well: "God made us without us, but he will not save us without us." We must cooperate with God's grace in order for it to be effective in us; we will not be possessed, our wills overtaken. This cooperation is an act of the will. God does not need our cooperation in order to act, but he wants it.

19. Did the children keep the first apparition a secret?

Only briefly. That very evening, Jacinta could not contain herself and excitedly told her mother, Olimpia, everything they had seen that day. At first, Olimpia thought Jacinta was playing a game, but when Francisco corroborated her story, she became concerned, though still unconvinced. Word spread throughout the town very quickly.

20. Did the families of the children believe them?

After the first apparition, the children agreed they would tell no one. But Jacinta told her mother, Olimpia, first.

Olimpia did not believe her, and neither did her many siblings. Francisco corroborated her story, but this did not make a difference; they still did not believe. Their father, Ti Marto, was the only member of their family to believe them. Jacinta and Francisco were mocked and ridiculed; they became the laughing stock of the village. Word spread so quickly that Lucia's parents first found out from a third party.

Lucia's father was not particularly religious and by all accounts did not feel strongly about the matter. Lucia's mother, Maria Rosa, was furious. She was convinced that her daughter was making the story up, trying to trick everyone. She took Lucia to see their pastor, Father Ferreira, because she thought he could get her daughter to admit she was lying.

The Santos family's situation did not help Maria Rosa's reaction to the news about the apparitions. The family's farm was suffering; their only son, Manuel, had been called up by the army and was training to fight in the trenches; Maria Rosa was overwhelmed, stressed, and run down. She was not disposed to hear a tale about visions of Our Lady.

21. Did Father Ferreira believe the children?

Father Ferreira's reaction was pragmatic. When Maria Rosa brought Lucia to the priest, she expected him to force the "truth" out of her, getting her to admit that the whole thing was a hoax. However, after hearing her account, he did not reject it. He recommended waiting and seeing what happened; after all, the Lady said she would come back on the thirteenth of every month. In fact, contrary to what Maria Rosa expected, Father Ferreira said the children should be allowed to continue going to the Cova da Iria.

As time went on, however, he became increasingly frustrated with the sort of attention the apparitions were garnering for their little town; because of the already anti-clerical, anti-Catholic attitude and practices of the government, he worried that this prominence would make them a target for persecution.

After the June 13 apparition, Father Ferreira sent for the children so he could question them. Lucia was apprehensive, but her cousins encouraged her, and they went filled with hope. To their surprise, Father Ferreira was kind and gentle, although the interview was interminable for the children. By the end, he was still not convinced. At this point, he told the children to be cautious, because it could be the devil playing a trick. This comment would have a devastating effect on Lucia, as we will see in question 26.

Father Ferreira showed a certain amount of frustration at the whole situation, but he usually treated the children and their parents with kindness and care. When, in August, the children were kidnapped and held by a government administrator (see question 50), that official tried to draw the ire of the masses away from himself by claiming Father Ferreira as an accomplice. The priest issued a response in the newspaper, vehemently denying any involvement. In the letter, he also stated that the reason he was not going to the Cova da Iria for the apparitions was that he wanted to avoid any appearance that he was instigating the visions.

22. Did the children know it was Our Lady who was appearing to them? Did they suspect who it was?

After the first apparition, the children did not know just who had come to visit them. They had been visited by the Angel of Peace the previous year, and he looked nothing like this woman. She told them she came from heaven, but said she would tell them who she was at a later date. When talking about her, the children simply called her "the Lady" or "the beautiful lady from heaven".

23. Did others think this was supposed to be Mary, whether the story was real or invented?

That seems to have been the general consensus. The children simply referred to her as "the Lady" or something similar. However, it appears that many—if not most—people did come to the conclusion that it must be the Blessed Mother. However, she did not identify herself until the final apparition in October.

THE JUNE APPARITION

24. What happened during the second apparition of Our Lady?

As June 13 came nearer, the children prepared to return to the Cova da Iria at the appointed time. Their mothers tried to convince them to stay home that day. After all, it was the feast of Saint Anthony of Padua. Anthony is a special patron of Portugal, since he was born in Lisbon, and his feast day meant a great celebration throughout the country, especially in Fatima, where the parish church was named for him. The children adored parties and celebrations such as this, so their mothers encouraged them to come to the festivities rather than returning to the Cova. But it was no use; they were going to see the Lady.

Since word had begun to spread already, there was a small group waiting for them at the Cova. A few accompanied them from the town, including Lucia's father, Antonio. There were some fifty to sixty people at the Cova. While they waited, they prayed the Rosary, after which the Lady appeared on the holm oak tree. Lucia asked again, "What do you want of me?" The woman responded with a list of requests. First, she wanted the children to come back again on July 13. Second, she wanted them to pray the Rosary every day. Third, she wanted Lucia to learn how to read and write; Our Lady told Lucia that she was to spend her life spreading devotion to her Immaculate Heart, so it was important for her to be literate. Then Lucia asked for healing for a young boy, as question 25 explains.

After this, Lucia asked if the Lady would take the three children to heaven. She responded that, yes, Jacinta and Francisco would go to heaven soon, but that Lucia needed to stay longer, because Jesus wished for her to help him make his mother known and loved and to establish devotion to her Immaculate Heart. She told Lucia that she would not be alone after her cousins went to heaven, because "I will never forsake you." Again, she opened her hands and the children were enveloped in light. They saw Jacinta and Francisco in light rising up to heaven, and Lucia in light that spread over the earth.

Lastly, they saw the Lady's heart, surrounded with thorns that pierced it and made it bleed. They understood the thorns to be sins, causing great suffering to her. The children were eager to offer their own sufferings as reparation for these sins.

25. Did any physical healings take place at the Cova during the apparitions?

A young crippled boy was healed, but this was not accomplished during the apparition itself. As she typically did during the apparitions, on June 13 Lucia asked the Lady for favors on behalf of the people, including the physical healing of a boy named João Carreira, who could not walk. Our Lady responded that he would be healed during the year, if he was converted. He was, in fact, healed, and served as a sacristan at the Fatima sanctuary church for almost fifty years.

26. Did the children ever doubt themselves?
Did they ever think they were hallucinating
or being deceived by the devil?

Lucia experienced a great deal of doubt before the July 13 apparition. She had been brought to speak with Father Ferreira, who told her to be cautious because these apparitions could be something from the devil, insisting that the devil could disguise himself and deceive the children.

This caused great suffering for Lucia. She had terrible doubts; nightmares plagued her in which the devil laughed at her because he had tricked her, dragging her down into hell. As a matter of fact, she had made up her mind *not to go* to the Cova da Iria on July 13, telling Francisco and Jacinta that they would have to speak to the Lady themselves.

Francisco and Jacinta prayed and tried to comfort her. Even the morning of July 13, she was determined not to go, but something compelled her to, some force from inside told her she must be there.

*27. Did the bishop come to Aljustrel to interview
the children?*

No, the bishop did not come out to question and inter-
rogate the children. While this is depicted in the 2020
film *Fatima*, probably to heighten the sense of the delicate position in which the apparitions put the Church,
the only ecclesiastical authorities who questioned the
children were Father Ferreira and some other priests.

*28. Did people come to the homes of the visionaries,
seeking favors from the Lady?*

Yes, the homes of the children were inundated with
admirers and those who wanted them to ask favors of
the Lady, to ask for her intercession. The influx of visitors was so dramatic that Lucia's father would often
simply go to the tavern after work and not return home
until he could be sure that no visitors remained. Maria
Rosa suffered greatly at this and was very bitter. Because
she did not believe her daughter was telling the truth,
Maria Rosa did not even have the consolation of knowing it was real.

*29. Did many people come to the Cova da Iria for the
apparitions? What sorts of people came, and why?*

News of the apparitions—or the *supposed* apparitions—
spread rapidly and widely. With each successive month,

the crowds grew. The crowds were composed of all sorts of people. There were certainly a great number of those who believed the children and wanted to see if they could catch a glimpse of the Lady, ask for her intercession, or ask the children to request favors of her. There were also some who attended out of sheer curiosity, wanting to see for themselves what all the commotion was about. And certainly, there were those who came to the Cova in order to mock the children and the pilgrims, who wanted simply to ridicule religious belief and fervor. It is interesting to note, however, that after the "Miracle of the Sun" (see question 61), many of these latter sort were converted themselves.

THE JULY APPARITION
AND THE THREE SECRETS

*30. What happened during the third apparition
of Our Lady?*

Word about these shepherd children and their alleged
apparitions was traveling fast. Many believed them, but
many doubted. A crowd of around 4,000 was gathered
at the Cova da Iria on July 13. Our Lady appeared above
the holm oak tree, and Lucia asked her, "What do you
want of me?" She responded that she wanted the children to continue to come on the thirteenth day of every
month and to pray the Rosary daily. She again emphasized the importance of the Rosary for world peace,
adding that it should be prayed "in honor of Our Lady
of the Rosary", because "only she can help you."

Lucia then brought up the disbelief and ridicule they
were facing and the hurt it was causing them. She asked
the Lady to tell them who she was and asked for a miracle so that everyone would believe. The Lady responded
that during the October apparition, she would reveal
her identity and perform a miracle.

After this, Lucia requested favors for the many people
who had sought her intercession—people at the apparition site, people who came to the children's homes. Our

Lady said they would need to pray the Rosary in order to obtain the graces they were requesting.

After this, Our Lady pleaded with the children to make sacrifices for the sake of the conversion of sinners. She told them to pray, "O Jesus, it is for love of you, for the conversion of sinners, and in reparation for the sins committed against the Immaculate Heart of Mary." As she finished saying this, she opened her hands from which light streamed. Then the children had a remarkable vision, detailed in question 33.

31. Why is the third apparition so important?

The July apparition contains the heart and the core of the message of Our Lady: there will be much suffering, but her Immaculate Heart will be victorious, and we must trust in God and make reparation for our sins. This particular apparition has also been the subject of the most scrutiny, speculation, and controversy.

In this apparition, Our Lady referred to some of the most important and earth-changing events that were to come: not only the end of the present war, but the start of another war; the errors of Russia and Communism, and the spread of those errors throughout the world; persecutions of the Church; and more.

The children experienced three visions, utterly profound, moving, even disturbing. Our Lady gave them these visions in order to help them understand the importance of converting sinners, and of converting the whole world. She told them not to tell anyone just yet what they had seen; because of this, they became known as the "Three Secrets of Fatima".

32. What are the Secrets of Fatima?

The so-called "Secrets of Fatima" are a series of visions Our Lady gave to Lucia, Jacinta, and Francisco during the July 13 apparition; at the end of the visions, she charged them not to tell anyone yet what they had seen. We do not know just why Our Lady told the children to keep the visions a secret. It could be because they dealt with events of the future; it could be because it simply was not the right time for the world to know. Years later, when Lucia was asked by her bishop to reveal the secrets, she first sought permission from Our Lady in prayer.

33. What is the First Secret of Fatima?

The first part of the vision mentioned above became known as the "First Secret" of Fatima. The rays of light from Our Lady's hands seemed to penetrate the earth itself, according to Lucia. They saw a sea of fire, with demons and human souls submerged in it, plunged into its depths; the souls were blackened, and sometimes thrown through the air by flames and clouds of smoke. The air was filled with shrieks and groans, the despair of each soul almost palpable. The demons were terrifying to behold. The children looked to Our Lady for relief, who said sadly, "You have seen hell, where the souls of poor sinners go. To save them, God wishes to establish in the world devotion to my Immaculate Heart. If what I say to you is done, many souls will be saved, and there will be peace."

Although the witnesses had no idea what the children had seen, the terror was clear on their faces. Lucia once said that if Our Lady had not already told the children they were going to heaven, they would have died of fright from this vision. After this vision, Our Lady taught the children the now famous "Fatima Prayer".

34. What is the Fatima Prayer?

"O, my Jesus, forgive us our sins. Save us from the fires of hell. Lead all souls to heaven, especially those most in need of your mercy." During the third apparition of Our Lady to the children, on July 13, 1917, she gave them this prayer and asked that it be said during the Holy Rosary at the end of each "decade", following the Glory Be (see question 98 on the Rosary). The children learned many prayers through the apparitions, both from the Angel of Peace and from Our Lady. This is the best known and most widely used.

35. What effect did the vision of the First Secret have on the children?

Lucia later wrote that, while they were all profoundly affected by the vision, Jacinta was especially moved by it. She was filled with such horror at the thought of souls suffering in this way that she accepted every suffering joyfully, knowing that it could help prevent souls from going to hell.

36. Why might Our Lady have shown the children such a terrifying vision?

The vision of hell was not for the children's sakes; they did not need it. They were living good and holy lives, striving for heaven and even making sacrifices for the sake of others. Our Lady had assured them they would be going to heaven. The vision was for the sake of others. Our Lady came to Fatima to lead men to God, to bring about reparation for sins and the conversion of sinners. This is why the children were shown this vision—for the sake of the whole world.

37. Is hell a real place? Is the devil real? Isn't that all just a medieval superstition?

On the contrary, according to Christianity, hell and the devil are all too real. Sacred Scripture, both the Old Testament and the New, assumes that the devil is real—the Book of Genesis, the Book of Job, Jesus' temptation in the desert, the demons who are cast out by Jesus. There are many places in Scripture, too, that speak of the eternal punishment or eternal fire. The Tradition of the Church has always recognized that hell is real and that the devil prowls about the world seeking the ruin of souls. Our Lady came to Fatima to save souls from that fate.

38. Were the children the first visionaries in history to have a vision of hell?

No, and as a matter of fact, visions of hell are reported quite often among visionaries, including a number of saints, such as Saint Teresa of Avila, Saint John Bosco, Saint Faustina Kowalska, Saint Catherine of Siena, Saint Hildegard of Bingen, and others. These visions all seem to have been for the same purpose: to chastise, to remind the visionary and the world of the reality of hell, and to warn against the sins that offend God.

39. Our Lady and the children talk a great deal about sin. What exactly is sin?

The *Catechism of the Catholic Church* describes sin as "an offense against reason, truth, and right conscience; it is failure in genuine love for God and neighbor caused by a perverse attachment to certain goods. It wounds the nature of man and injures human solidarity. It has been defined as 'an utterance, a deed, or a desire contrary to the eternal law'" (CCC 1849, quoting Saint Augustine).

40. What is the Second Secret?

Following the vision of hell came the Second Secret. As the vision was ending, Our Lady told the children that God wanted devotion to her Immaculate Heart to be established throughout the world, in order to save souls from hell. If this was done, she said, many souls would be saved, and peace would reign. Our Lady told the children that the war would end if this was done.

However, she said, if this was not done, an even worse war would break out during the pontificate of Pius XI. (At the time, the pope was Benedict XV, and there was no such thing yet as a Pope Pius XI.) Our Lady told of a sign that would precede this worse war: a night illumined by an unknown light, which would be a sign that God is about to punish the world for its crimes, through war, famine, and persecutions of the Church.

The idea of a war worse than the Great War would have been unthinkable at the time—but worse it would indeed turn out to be. During the papacy of Pius XI, the Second World War broke out, which would prove far more devastating than the First, affecting a much greater part of the world and resulting in the deaths of up to fifty million people, with numerous unspeakable atrocities.

The wars, famines, and persecutions of which Our Lady spoke she attributed to Communism, which that year was suddenly on the rise in Russia. She told the children that she would return at a later time to request that Russia be consecrated to her Immaculate Heart, as well as request the "Communion of Reparation" (or the First Saturdays Devotion, as it would later be called) (see question 75). She said that if her requests were heeded, Russia would be converted and there would be peace; if not, Russia would spread its errors throughout the world, which would result in even more wars, persecutions, and great suffering.

But, in the end, she told them, her Immaculate Heart would triumph.

*41. Our Lady said the First World War would
end "soon". It was over a year before it ended.
How can we explain this delay?*

By the time Our Lady announced the end, the war had
been raging for three years, ripping wounds across the
face of Europe, killing almost an entire generation of
young men. There was a bloody stalemate on the west-
ern front, with no end in sight. Indeed, for many people, it must have seemed at times like the war would
never end at all. For those who had loved ones in the
trenches—not to mention for the soldiers themselves—
every day likely felt like an eternity. In 1917, however,
the tide of the war began to turn with the arrival of
United States troops, and by July 1918, the Allied forces
began to draw the conflict to a close. The "soon" to
which Our Lady referred came on November 11, 1918,
the signing of the Armistice of Compiègne, just over
one year after the last apparition, although the war was
already effectively over by October 1918.

*42. Did the "unknown light in the sky" mentioned
in the vision actually precede the Second World War?*

An "unknown light" did occur in a remarkable fash-
ion just prior to the outset of the Second World War.
Between January 25 and 26, 1938, a tremendous aurora
borealis was visible throughout Europe and parts of
America, for a period of almost five hours. This phenomenon reached much farther south than it typically

does, astounding millions who had never seen anything like it. Lucia—by then a Dorothean nun—immediately saw in this the fulfillment of Our Lady's prophecy and knew that the terrible foretold war would soon come.

43. Didn't the Second World War start on September 1, 1939, when Germany invaded Poland, seven months after Pius XI died? Doesn't this mean Our Lady's prophecy was wrong?

There is legitimate debate among historians as to when the Second World War began. Many mark the beginning with the invasion of Poland by Germany on September 1, 1939. However, the fighting began prior to that: in 1937, Japan invaded Manchuria (today northeast China) and invaded Russia in 1938. Germany's annexation of Austria, and subsequent occupation, began on March 12, 1938. Some historians—and Sister Lucia—consider this the beginning of the Second World War in Europe, which was many months before the death of Pius XI on February 10, 1938.

44. What is the Third Secret?

Of the many facets of the Fatima apparitions, the Third Secret of Fatima is without question the source of the greatest controversy, speculation, and attention. It is the most symbolic and takes a good deal of analysis and unpacking. In contrast to the first two visions, Our

Lady did not speak during the Third Secret, leaving the images to speak for themselves.

First, the children saw an angel with a flaming sword. The flames looked as though they would set the world on fire, Lucia wrote, but Our Lady's radiance doused them. The angel pointed toward the earth and cried out, "Penance! Penance! Penance!"

Then the children found themselves enveloped in light, as they had during the May and June apparitions. They saw people walking up a steep mountain, with a large cross at the top. They beheld a bishop dressed in white, who seemed to them to be the pope, with other bishops, priests, and religious, going up the mountain. The pope passed through a ruined city, sorrowful and pained at what he was seeing, praying for the souls of those dead he saw. He dropped to his knees at the foot of the cross on top of the hill and was killed by a group of soldiers, who then killed those with him.

Beneath the arms of the cross were two angels, gathering up the blood of these martyrs, which they then sprinkled on the souls that were going to God.

After this vision ended, Our Lady departed.

45. When were the Secrets of Fatima revealed?

The children held the secrets closely, not divulging them to anyone, for many years. Jacinta and Francisco died without revealing them. Government officials, friends and family, onlookers, the curious—many, many people tried to extract the secrets from them.

In July 1941, when Lucia was a Dorothean nun, Bishop José Alves Correia da Silva of the diocese of Leiria (which contains Fatima) asked her to tell the world more about Jacinta. Lucia discerned that it was time to reveal the first two secrets, as this would allow her to explore and explain Jacinta's inner life, since they had such a profound effect on her. The text of the first two was sent to Bishop da Silva on August 31, 1941. She made some additions to this text on December 8, 1941. The Third Secret, though, she kept confidential.

On January 3, 1944, she wrote about the Third Secret. She did so at the request of the bishop of Leiria and after seeking in prayer the permission of Our Lady. Although she wrote it down, it was still to remain secret. It was put into a sealed envelope and entrusted to Bishop da Silva. On April 4, 1957, the still-sealed envelope was transferred to the secret archives of the Holy Office (which would later become the Congregation for the Doctrine of the Faith) at the Vatican. Multiple popes read the secret after that date and decided not to publish it. It was finally revealed on May 13, 2000, during the Mass of the beatification of Francisco and Jacinta at the Cova da Iria.

46. Who read the Third Secret before it was revealed publicly?

On August 17, 1959, the envelope containing the Third Secret was brought to Pope Saint John XXIII. He read the secret (along with Alfredo Cardinal Ottaviani and Archbishop Loris Capovilla), prayed about it, and decided not to reveal it. It was sealed and returned to the Holy Office. In fact, the Vatican released a statement saying that the secret would probably remain sealed forever. This was a major disappointment to the countless curious onlookers who had been waiting to discover the contents for so many years.

On March 27, 1965, Pope Saint Paul VI read the secret with Archbishop Angelo Dell'Acqua, and once again the pope decided not to publish it. It was again returned to the Holy Office, sealed.

Pope Saint John Paul II asked to read the Third Secret while he was in the hospital, recovering from the attempt on his life. He later decided to reveal the secret at Jacinta and Francisco's beatification.

47. Why was the Third Secret held for so long?

When Sister Lucia wrote down the Third Secret, she sealed it in an envelope and wrote that it was not to be opened before 1960 and was to be read by either the patriarch of Lisbon or the bishop of Leiria. She indicated that it could also be read at her death, if that came first. The date of 1960 was not set by Our Lady, but Lucia felt that it would allow time to understand the secret better. She also said that it was not her place to interpret it, but rather the pope's. Each successive pope who chose not to reveal the contents apparently thought it was not the opportune time to do so, although we cannot know for sure what their motivations were.

48. Was the Third Secret fully revealed?

Yes, it was. This is a somewhat controversial question—
as is just about everything related to the July apparition and the visions of the children. People have given
many objections over the years, citing evidence that the
Vatican did not release the entirety of (or even *any* of)
the true Third Secret. There is wild speculation, but
all of it falls flat. On several occasions, Sister Lucia herself verified the authenticity of the letter, its contents,
and its interpretation by Cardinal Ratzinger and others. After the secret was revealed at the beatification of
Jacinta and Francisco, she pulled no punches when she
said, "Everything has been published; there are no more
secrets." Perhaps the skeptics were disappointed with its
contents; the secrecy and delay led many people to spec-
ulate that the secret would contain some cataclysmic or
apocalyptic prophecies, so perhaps, by comparison, the
reality seems rather tame. But it is what it is: the Third
Secret has been fully revealed.

49. Is the Third Secret meant to be taken as a literal prediction of a future event?

Cardinal Joseph Ratzinger—then prefect of the Congregation for the Doctrine of the Faith, and later Pope
Benedict XVI—wrote an extensive theological commentary on the Third Secret to coincide with its release
in May 2000. Cardinal Ratzinger's commentary, given in
the Vatican document "The Message of Fatima", digs

into the symbolism contained in the imagery of the secret and analyzes it from a theological perspective, reading it as a parable of the Church's long suffering in the twentieth century and an urgent call to faith, hope, and love. The vision is highly symbolic, similar to the prophetic visions contained in Sacred Scripture. It is not meant to depict with photo-realism the way future events will play out, but to communicate spiritual facts, ideas, and lessons that God's people need to hear.

THE AUGUST AND
SEPTEMBER APPARITIONS

*50. Did government officials try to intervene to
prevent the August apparition?*

Yes, they did. Officials were becoming very nervous
about the way that the purported apparitions were affecting the people. They had hoped the children would be
revealed as charlatans by this point. Instead, there was
an increase in public religious fervor in response to the
apparitions, which seemed increasingly credible with
each passing month.

The hamlet of Aljustrel was part of the administrative
district of Ourem. The city council was headed by Artur
de Oliveira Santos, a journalist, who had been baptized a
Catholic but abandoned the faith and became one of the
most prominent Freemasons in the region. Santos was
fiercely anti-Catholic and wanted nothing more than to
bring an end to this business about the apparitions. The
Portuguese newspapers—typically anti-religious—were
critical of the authorities' response, finding it negligent
and ineffective. Santos took these criticisms very personally. He decided he had to put a stop to it and do
whatever he could to discredit the children and keep
people from going to the apparition site.

There was even more commotion after the children announced that the Lady had confided in them a secret. Santos was determined to get this secret out of the children.

On August 10, he summoned them to administrative council headquarters in Ourem. Although Lucia's family did not believe in the apparitions, her father, Antonio, was more sympathetic than the rest, and he accompanied her to the interview. Ti Marto—who did believe and encouraged the children to keep the secret—went along, but left his son and daughter at home, since he did not have a safe way to transport them the nine miles from Aljustrel to Ourem. Lucia and the other children expected that she would be given an ultimatum: either reveal the secret or die. Santos did, indeed, threaten her with many penalties, including death, but she would not budge. He even threatened severe civil penalties on the parents, but to no avail. The fathers were not fazed, which further enraged Santos. They returned home.

On August 13, Santos imprisoned the children in the local jail, as question 52 explains.

51. Were the children present at the Cova da Iria for the August 13 apparition?

No, they were prevented from being there. Santos continued his efforts to put an end to the dubious apparitions and took drastic measures on August 13. He went to the homes of the visionaries, claiming that he wanted to go with them to the apparition site. No one suspected deceit, and the children boarded his horse-drawn wagon to go to the Cova. But suddenly it sped off in another direction, toward Ourem.

More than 15,000 people had gathered at the Cova da Iria, the largest crowd yet. Something remarkable happened at noon when the children were not there. Witnesses said that, out of the east, a small cloud came and settled on top of the holm oak tree where the Lady usually appeared. The sun turned pale, and after a short while, the cloud departed and returned to the east.

52. What happened to the children in Ourem on August 13?

Back in Ourem, Councilman Santos brought the children to his home, pretending to bring them to the Cova to see the Lady. He spoke with them and tried to convince them to admit that the apparitions were a sham, that they were making it all up. Santos' wife was a devout Catholic, but she could not practice her faith openly for fear of her husband. She treated the children quite well, fed them good meals, and made them feel comfortable. They slept at the Santos home that night.

However, the next day, Santos changed tactics. He threatened them, then locked them up in the local jail. The children were frightened, and Jacinta in particular was hurt because she thought their parents had abandoned them. Francisco and Lucia tried to console her, as did the prisoners. One played music to try to cheer the children up; they began to dance, and Jacinta's dancing partner picked her up and danced with her in his arms, since she was so little. The children offered their sufferings for the conversion of sinners. They prayed fervently, and even got the prisoners to pray along with them.

Santos threatened to throw each of them alive into a vat of boiling oil. They took the threat very seriously, convinced he was telling the truth. But they remained resolute, never budging.

After three days, on August 15, Santos had the children dropped off at the parish rectory and returned home.

53. When the children were imprisoned, did a great crowd (including their parents) gather outside the jail, calling for their release?

No, but the people of Aljustrel were very upset at what the government was doing, as can be seen from the townspeople's reaction when the children were eventually returned home on August 15. Had it not been for Ti Marto's intervention, the angry mob would likely have mauled Father Ferreira, who they thought was a conspirator in the whole matter. The priest maintained his innocence, but the crowd was very upset over the government's actions and could almost not be contained.

54. Did the imprisonment affect how Lucia's family felt about the apparitions?

Unfortunately, no. Lucia had suffered a great deal from her family's disbelief. Her mother was so convinced that her daughter was lying that she would threaten and beat her. After Father Ferreira's interviews did not convince Lucia to admit her deception, Maria Rosa hoped that the administrator would be able to do so. When Artur de Oliveira Santos summoned the children in August, Maria Rosa gladly sent Lucia along with her husband and Ti Marto.

After the children were imprisoned, missed the August 13 apparition, and were finally returned home, Lucia's family showed no great relief, or even welcome. She was sent out with the sheep, just the same as a normal day. Lucia never felt resentful or angry about this; it hurt her terribly, but she knew that God would make the best come out of it and that her suffering could be offered for the conversion of sinners.

55. Did Our Lady ever appear to the children in August? What happened?

Once the children returned home, they got back into their routine, including caring for the sheep. On Sunday, August 19, they were grazing their flocks at Valinhos, about a ten-minute walk from Aljustrel, where the Angel of Peace had appeared to them twice. Around 4:00 P.M., Lucia had a sense that Our Lady would soon appear, and shortly thereafter they saw the familiar flash of light. Jacinta was not with them at the time, but the moment she arrived, Our Lady appeared standing upon a holm oak tree. This was the only time Our Lady appeared to them outside of the Cova da Iria.

This apparition was shorter than the others. After Lucia's customary question—"What do you want of me?"—Our Lady responded that she wanted the children to continue going to the Cova da Iria on the thirteenth of every month and to continue praying the Rosary every day. She also told them that she would perform a miracle in October during the apparition, so that everyone would believe that she was really appearing to them. She said that the miracle would have been even more spectacular, had it not been for the abhorrent behavior of the government officials.

After some more questions, the apparition ended with Lucia asking for more favors and healings. Our Lady said she would cure some during the year. Then her face suddenly became sad, and she asked the children to pray very much and make sacrifices for sinners; many souls go to hell, she said, because no one prays or makes sacrifices for them. Then she left the children, to see them again the following month.

56. How did the Church throughout Portugal react to the apparitions as they were occurring?

The events in Fatima were becoming very widely known and were causing quite a bit of controversy. The secularist newspapers were running articles mocking the putative apparitions, the children, and the village. Priests throughout the country were quite anxious about what might come as a result of these events. Already before the events at Fatima, the Church was, at best, tolerated by the Portuguese government (see question 8), and the plan of most priests seemed to be to fly under the radar and avoid detection until absolutely necessary. For most clerics in Portugal, their stance on Fatima was that it was probably a hallucination at best or duplicitous at worst, and that the faithful should just avoid the topic altogether. The conflict between the Church and the government in 1917 was mostly a war of words and of attrition. It was a fragile situation, and something as explosive as these apparitions could upset the delicate balance.

Jesuit Father Francisco Cruz was a highly regarded and experienced priest; he had been the visiting priest at Saint Anthony in Fatima who interviewed Lucia and allowed her to receive her First Holy Communion at a younger age than normal. He decided to go to Fatima to interview the children himself. After speaking with them, he believed that the apparitions were real, which helped bolster the children's reputation of credibility.

57. What happened at the fifth apparition on September 13?

Ironically, and contrary to the intentions of the authorities, the imprisonment of the children in August created a great deal of interest in the apparitions. Even among disbelievers and anti-religious zealots throughout the country, people believed that Artur Santos had acted inappropriately, and this just helped spread the word even more.

It is estimated that around 25,000 to 30,000 people came to the Cova da Iria for the apparition on September 13, 1917. The children could barely get through the crowd to get to where they needed to be. As they made their way through, great throngs of people pleaded with them to ask the Lady to grant their petitions.

The children began to pray the Rosary with the people and soon saw the familiar flash of lightning, after which the Lady appeared above the holm oak tree. Lucia asked, "What do you want of me?" The Lady responded that she wanted them to pray the Rosary for an end to the war. She also told the children that, during the October apparition, the children would see Jesus, Our Lady of Sorrows, Our Lady of Mount Carmel, and Saint Joseph holding the child Jesus.

Now, the children had enthusiastically taken upon themselves all sorts of sacrifices and suffering, for the conversion of sinners and the reparation of sins that had been committed. But the Lady cautioned them against going too far, saying that God is pleased with their sacrifices, but that they must be reasonable.

The apparition ended, as usual, with Lucia offering the petitions of the multitude to the Lady.

THE OCTOBER APPARITION
AND THE MIRACLE
OF THE SUN

58. The Lady had promised that she would tell the children who she was and perform a miracle during the October apparition. What were people expecting?

The crowds at the Cova da Iria had been growing rapidly each month. All over the country, people were telling stories about the shepherd children in Fatima who were speaking with a woman from heaven. All sorts of people—believers, nonbelievers, the curious, the disdainful, the supportive, the mocking—came to see. The secular government and anti-clerical newspapers were expecting a huge letdown for the believers; they expected no miracle, which would cause tremendous outrage among the people, and possibly even a violent reaction against the self-proclaimed seers.

Believers, on the other hand, expected exactly what the Lady had said. They expected that she would tell them who she was indeed—Mary, the Mother of Our Lord—and that she would perform a spectacular miracle for all to see and believe.

59. Was there opposition in the weeks before October 13?

Just as in the months before, there were many forces at work against the children in the lead-up to the October apparition. The government, fully expecting nothing miraculous to happen and the whole affair to be exposed as a hoax, was certain that the failure of the apparition would result in a loss of faith among the people and irreparable damage to the Church's reputation. Officials and journalists continued openly to mock and try to discredit the apparitions and the visionaries. Their secularist agenda held that there was nothing at all to religion and that science, which they erroneously saw as contradictory to religion, held all the answers.

Even the children's neighbors in Aljustrel were, by and large, skeptical about the apparitions. There was a great deal of hostility toward the children and their families on the part of these neighbors. This brings to mind the words of Jesus that prophets are not without honor except in their native land and indeed in their own homes (cf. Mt 13:57).

Right up to this final apparition, family members, priests, neighbors, and others continually tried to convince the children to admit that they had made it all up, that it was a fraud. Part of their motivation was fear: people were growing afraid of what might happen to the children if nothing miraculous occurred at the Cova. In fact, on October 12, the day before the apparition, Maria Rosa took Lucia to the church for confession, so worried was she that the crowds would kill her daughter and the rest of them. Even though she remained skeptical, she was resolved to face whatever fate awaited her daughter.

The children remained steadfast. They did not lose faith, did not waver. The Lady had told them she would come, and she would not deceive them—so they believed completely.

60. *What happened at the sixth apparition?*

There was great anticipation leading up to the sixth and final apparition. The crowd was massive—anywhere from 70,000 to 90,000 people at the Cova da Iria and the surrounding areas. It had been pouring rain for more than a day, and everything was drenched. But that did not deter the people. They came trudging through the mud to get to the apparition site.

Because of the crowd, the children had a difficult time reaching the holm oak. Once they got there, Lucia asked everyone to pray the Rosary. The children saw that familiar flash of light, and suddenly there stood the Lady on the holm oak. Lucia began, as she always did, with the question "What do you want of me?" This time, the Lady responded more specifically than she had in previous months: she said that she wanted a chapel built on that site in her honor. She also said that the war would end and soldiers would soon return to their homes.

The Lady also answered a question that had been plaguing the children and curious onlookers since May when the apparitions began and that she had promised in July to answer on this day. "I am the Lady of the

Rosary," she told the children. There was no question what this meant: this was Mary, the mother of Jesus, the Mother of God, the Lady who guides the world to her son. She asked them to continue praying the Rosary every day.

As usual, Lucia then brought the petitions of the people to Our Lady, who responded that those who seek blessings from God must ask forgiveness of their sins and reform their lives. Then Our Lady made a plea to the children, one they must share with the whole world. Looking sad, she said, "Do not offend the Lord our God anymore, because He is already so much offended."

61. What was the Miracle of the Sun?

As the October 13 apparition came to an end and Our Lady was about to leave, she opened her hands as she ascended. Her light was projected onto the sun, and Lucia cried out, "Look at the sun!" Then came the miracle that Our Lady had promised, the miracle that would make people believe the children were really speaking with the Blessed Virgin Mary.

The rain, which had been pouring all night, had stopped. Everything was a soaked, sopping, muddy mess. Suddenly, the sun appeared to spin rapidly; its color became dull and opaque, and it cast multicolored lights across the land and people below. The sun jerked from its position and "danced" around, zigzagging all over the sky. The crowd stood and marveled, eyes fixed on the heavens, as this display continued for several

minutes. Then all at once the sun appeared to careen
and plummet toward the earth. Many in the crowd seem
to have thought this was the end of the world; they
dropped to their knees in the mud, begging forgiveness
for their sins and praising the Mother of God. The sun
then returned to its position in the sky. Everything—the
ground, the people's clothes—was suddenly completely
dry. All told, the Miracle of the Sun lasted more than
ten minutes.

During the Miracle of the Sun, there were many
miraculous healings among the people assembled: blind
people who could now see, lame people who could
now walk, not to mention many conversions. These
were further manifestations of the miraculous nature of
Our Lady's apparitions.

There were somewhere between 50,000 and 70,000
people at the Cova itself that day, witnessing the Miracle of the Sun. There are even many people beyond the
Cova who witnessed it, from as far as thirty miles away.
Not everyone who was there thought he had witnessed
a miracle; some thought it was just some sort of abnor-
mal meteorological phenomenon or else had some other
purely rational explanation. There were many converted
that day—many believers whose faith was strengthened,
many skeptics who became believers—but, yes, there
were many who steadfastly and stubbornly refused to
accept what they had clearly seen with their own eyes
alongside tens of thousands of others. As was famously
said in regards to Our Lady's apparition at Lourdes: For
those with faith, no explanation is necessary. For those
without faith, no explanation is possible.

62. Are there contemporary reports from witnesses of the Miracle of the Sun?

Yes, there are a great number of reports from eyewitnesses who observed the Miracle of the Sun, many of whom recorded detailed accounts of their experiences.

One such eyewitness was a woman named Mary Allen. We do not know much about her, but she said that shortly after arriving at the Cova, she saw a bright light, the rain suddenly ceased, and the clouds opened up to reveal a sun brighter and larger than our own, but she was able to look at it without pain. She tells of the sun spinning, shooting streams of light, and plummeting toward the earth. People began to throw themselves to the ground and pray the Act of Contrition, she writes. Afterward, the ground and all of their clothes were bone dry.

Ti Marto, father of Jacinta and Francisco, gave his own account. He also said that they could look directly at the sun with ease and without pain, and it seemed to flicker on and off. It seemed to shoot out bands of multicolored light; then it danced about in the sky, until it seemed to hurtle toward the earth.

Another man, named Alfredo da Silva Santos, came from Lisbon and was very skeptical about the apparitions. He reported seeing the Miracle of the Sun as well; the sun appeared to be detached from the sky, he said, and plummeted toward the earth.

One of the most interesting sources on the Miracle of the Sun is the pro-government, anti-clerical, anti-Catholic newspaper *O Seculo*. The paper had a very large readership in Lisbon and the surrounding area. Avelino de Almeida of *O Seculo* had been writing negatively and derisively about the apparitions for months and was on hand to report on what he was sure would be a fiasco, a big letdown, and on the ensuing wrath of the crowd. He reported the same details as others: you could look at the sun without discomfort or pain; the sun shook, zigzagged around the sky, in violation of all physical laws.

And there are many more such accounts.

63. Might the miracle have been simply a mass hallucination, or the power of suggestion, or collusion for a hoax?

There is no evidence to indicate that this was a mass hallucination, a hoax, or anything of the sort. All of the facts of the matter point to the *extreme unlikelihood* of anything but a miraculous event. The vastness of the crowd would have made it impossible to collaborate or collude on any sort of hoax. A number of unbelievers, including secular, anti-Catholic newspapers and others, wrote about the event. No one was expecting a solar miracle specifically, so there is no reason to think 70,000 people would hallucinate the same image and effects. Many people outside of the Cova da Iria witnessed the Miracle of the Sun as well.

64. Were there witnesses of the Miracle of the Sun beyond the Cova da Iria?

One of the most fascinating points to make about the Miracle of the Sun—and a point that seems to support its veracity—is the fact that there were witnesses *beyond the Cova da Iria*. People from miles around reported seeing it.

To take one example: A young man sat in school, about six miles away from Fatima. There was a loud cry from the villagers outside, so the teacher and pupils rushed outside. They witnessed the sun making wild and erratic movements, zigzagging and even seeming to crash toward the earth. The young man recalled one fellow villager who had mocked the faithful making their way to Fatima but now stood there stunned, staring at the sky, shaking with fear, and finally falling to the ground crying out, "Holy Virgin, Holy Virgin".

There is a very similar story from a boy named Inacio Lourenco, in a village about twelve miles from Fatima; a commotion outside the school drew the teacher and students out, and they observed the Miracle of the Sun. A poet named Afonso Lopes Vieira lived more than thirty miles from Fatima, and he also recorded witnessing the miracle.

There were even reports from a British ship that was sailing off the coast of Portugal. With no context, not even realizing that these apparitions were happening (let alone expecting any sort of miracle), the sailors saw the miracle and were perplexed and frightened.

65. Did the children also witness the Miracle of the Sun?

No, the children witnessed a unique apparition only visible to the three of them. After Our Lady had disappeared, beside the sun the children saw a vision of

Saint Joseph holding the child Jesus. Next to them was
Our Lady, clothed in white with a blue mantle. Saint
Joseph and Jesus traced the Sign of the Cross, appearing to bestow their blessing upon the world. After this
image disappeared, Lucia saw Jesus and Mary, in the
appearance of Our Lady of Sorrows. Jesus once again
blessed the world. Then, lastly, Mary took the form
of Our Lady of Mount Carmel, a sort of prefiguration of
Lucia's eventual entrance into the Carmel at Coimbra.
All three children saw the vision of the Holy Family,
but the last two were only visible to Lucia.

66. Were the secular authorities in Portugal supportive of the children throughout the time of the apparitions?

No. The secular authorities were not supportive of
Lucia, Francisco, and Jacinta, and at times they dealt
with them ruthlessly, even physically restraining them
and treating them like criminals, as in the case of Artur
de Oliveira Santos (see question 50). That is how
important it was to these authorities to discredit the
visionaries. The secular governmental authorities had
nothing but contempt for the Catholic Church and
her members and adherents. They wanted to crush
the Church, and some members of the government
bragged that their policies would ensure an elimination of priests in the country, and elimination of the
Church altogether. As word spread around the region
and across Portugal (and more) about these supposed

apparitions, the anti-Catholic government deliberately fought the children and their growing base of support. The tactics of the government were so drastic that even the secular, anti-religious press was critical of what they were doing.

FATIMA AFTER THE APPARITIONS

*67. What happened in the months following
the Miracle of the Sun?*

The secular authorities had done what they could to
keep these apparitions from enflaming religious fervor,
but they failed. Thousands upon thousands of people
had flocked to the Cova da Iria, and tens of thousands
witnessed one of the most profound and awe-inspiring
miracles of the twentieth century. But the authorities
continued to try to cover up the events at Fatima.

After December 1918, armed guards were sent to the
Cova da Iria to quash the growing enthusiasm for these
apparitions. A small pilgrimage chapel had been constructed by local Catholics (see questions 69–70). No
matter what the authoritarian, anti-Catholic government officials did, pilgrims kept coming.

*68. How do we know so much about the apparitions,
including what Our Lady said?*

There are several sources that tell us what happened
in Fatima over a century ago. The primary, and most
complete and invaluable, resource is the memoirs of

Sister Lucia, which she wrote off and on for many years. Sister Lucia lived to the age of ninety-seven, dying in 2005; but many decades before, when she was in her twenties, she began to record in great detail those most fateful events of her childhood. This is where we find personal information on the interactions between the visionaries, what was in their hearts and minds throughout all of this, and, perhaps most importantly, what the Angel of Peace and Our Lady said during their apparitions.

Other details were provided by eyewitnesses and by those who came to the Cova da Iria, lived in the town, went to the parish, or knew the visionaries and their families. The family members of the visionaries passed stories down. There are many newspaper articles; there are memoirs and other records of people who were peripherally involved with the events but still have a great deal of information to contribute.

69. Was a chapel built at the Cova da Iria, in response to Our Lady's request?

Yes. On April 28, 1919, construction of a simple chapel was begun at the Cova da Iria, to fulfill Our Lady's request and provide a place of worship for the many pilgrims who were coming to the site. This was done unofficially: Church authorities were not involved. The first Mass officially celebrated in the chapel was on October 13, 1921, the fourth anniversary of the final apparition.

The cornerstone for what would become the Basilica of Our Lady of the Rosary was laid on May 13, 1928. Construction was not completed until 1954. The church was consecrated on October 7, 1953, and in November 1954 Pope Pius XII designated the church a basilica.

Over the years, this has developed into a complex of several buildings, known collectively as the Sanctuary of Our Lady of Fatima. This includes the Basilica of Our Lady of the Rosary, the Chapel of the Lausperene, the Chapel of the Apparitions, and more.

70. Why did Mary ask for a chapel to be built there?

When Our Lady appeared at Fatima, she made it a holy place. It has become a site of pilgrimage, with up to twenty million people flocking to Fatima every year to see where Our Lady appeared to the shepherd children, to visit the tombs of the visionaries, to celebrate Mass, to pray. For many Christians, going on pilgrimage to holy sites makes the tenets of our faith that much more tangible. Our Lady knew that people would come, and she knew they would need a chapel (which would develop into a magnificent shrine) to accommodate them.

When she appeared to Saint Bernadette at Lourdes, she requested that a chapel be built so that people could come and pray and bathe in the miraculous waters there. At Tepeyac Hill in Mexico City, Our Lady of Guadalupe told Saint Juan Diego to tell the bishop a chapel should be constructed in her honor.

71. Where did the famous "Pilgrim Virgin Statue" of Fatima, which travels around the world, come from?

José Ferreira Thedim was a sculptor who was asked in 1919 to carve a statue depicting Our Lady of Fatima. This work was commissioned by Gilberto Fernandes dos Santos (no relation to Lucia), a man who believed passionately in the apparitions and had a great devotion to Our Lady of Fatima. Thedim accepted the invitation and worked with Lucia to construct an accurate representation of Our Lady. After speaking with Lucia, he became a firm believer in the veracity of the apparitions, and the sculpting became a devotional practice for him. When Lucia saw the statue at its completion, she wept with happiness. In May 1920, it was placed in the small pilgrimage chapel (see questions 69–70) and would later travel the world.

72. What happened to Francisco after the apparitions ended?

The experiences of the apparitions changed Francisco's life, as one would expect. One year after the Miracle of the Sun, Jacinta contracted the Spanish flu, and Francisco contracted the same disease shortly thereafter.

Francisco longed to go to heaven. When he was asked what he wanted to be when he grew up, he would always respond that he just wanted to go to heaven. When the government officials threatened to boil him in oil if he did not deny the truth of the apparitions, he willingly accepted the possibility of death. Death was not something he feared: he had been assured by Our Lady that he would be going to heaven, and he wanted his illness to be a means for making reparation for sinners, offering his suffering for their sake.

Francisco loved to go to the church to pray. His favorite spot was behind the altar at the foot of the tabernacle, where he could be hidden, private, and close to Jesus in the Blessed Sacrament. He would also separate himself from the others on occasion while they were grazing their sheep; in these private moments, he would meditate and reflect on what Our Lady had said to them and shown them during her apparitions, and he would pray fervently.

During his illness, he always appeared joyful, even cheerful in his acceptance of the suffering, of the sickness that would fulfill Our Lady's promise to bring him to heaven soon. Paradoxically, the very fact that he was suffering so much is what helped him have such great joy in the face of his suffering. He knew that his suffering was doing good, offering it as he did for the conversion of sinners and the consolation of the Lord, in reparation for the offenses of sin. He knew that, before long, he would be going to heaven.

As his death drew near, he asked for the sacrament of confession and to receive Holy Communion. Although during the third apparition of the Angel of Peace Francisco had once drunk the Precious Blood from the angel's chalice (see question 15), he had never received his First Holy Communion in church. He asked Lucia to pray that he would be able to receive these sacraments, and indeed he was. He received the Sacred Host on his deathbed, the day before he died.

Francisco died on April 4, 1919, and was buried in the cemetery of Saint Anthony in Fatima. On March 12, 1952, his remains were transferred to a side chapel at the basilica that had been constructed in the Cova da Iria.

73. What happened to Jacinta after the apparitions ended?

After the apparitions of Our Lady ended, Jacinta remained fixated on saving sinners. The vision of hell in the July 13 apparition profoundly changed her, and she was determined to do whatever she could to keep people out of hell, including offering up her own suffering for their conversion.

Jacinta had always loved nature. She dearly loved her sheep, giving them names and caring for them. Once she tried to carry one home on her shoulders, after seeing an image of the Good Shepherd doing the same. After the apparitions, she called the sun "Our Lady's lamp" and the stars "the angels' lanterns".

At times, she could be stubborn and self-centered, but she was very intelligent and sensitive. This maturity of spirit made her very receptive to Our Lady's message, and Lucia later said that of the three children, Jacinta seemed to have been the most affected by the apparitions. She made the salvation of souls her primary goal in life, and many people reported receiving favors through her intercession and prayers.

Jacinta was blessed to become a powerful intercessor. Many miracles are attributed to her prayers and intercessions. In one instance, prior to her death, it seems that she even bilocated. She was at home, praying for a young man who was lost in the woods on his way home, during a storm; the young man stopped where he was, knelt, and prayed, and Jacinta appeared and led him to safety.

In October 1918, Jacinta contracted the Spanish flu. When Francisco became ill shortly thereafter, she worried much more about him than about herself. She suffered a great deal watching him suffer, and when he died, she would have given anything to see him again.

Our Lady appeared to Jacinta during her illness and told her that Francisco would soon go to heaven—but she asked if Jacinta wanted to remain on earth longer, in order to suffer more for the conversion of sinners. Jacinta, of course, said yes. She developed bronchial pneumonia and was sent to the hospital in Ourem. After almost two months, she returned home with a large chest wound and tuberculosis.

Our Lady continued to visit Jacinta, bringing her comfort and saying that she would soon come to bring Jacinta to heaven. She was moved around to more hospitals, offering all of her suffering for the conversion of sinners and the good of the Holy Father. Lucia was heartbroken at the suffering of her cousin, especially after having lost Francisco. But Jacinta told Lucia that she must stay and tell the world that God wants devotion to the Immaculate Heart of Mary.

After a successful surgery, for some reason that her doctors could not discern, Jacinta's health deteriorated.

She was moved to a hospital in the capital city of Lisbon. On the evening of February 20, Jacinta knew that she would die. She asked to be given the last rites, so Father José Pereira dos Reis came to administer the sacraments to her. After she made her confession, Father promised to bring her Holy Communion in the morning. (Remember that, like Francisco, she had drunk from the chalice of the Angel of Peace—see question 15— but had not yet received her First Holy Communion in church.) When Jacinta told the priest that she would die that night and asked to be given sacred Viaticum right away, he assured her that he would be back in the morning.

Jacinta died a few hours later, on February 20, 1920. She was initially buried in a cemetery in Ourem. In 1935, her remains were moved to Saint Anthony in Fatima, near her brother Francisco. On March 1, 1951, her remains were exhumed and found to be preserved. She was then placed in a side chapel at the basilica.

74. Did Our Lady tell Jacinta anything before she died?

While Jacinta was at her final hospital, in Lisbon, just before she died, Our Lady visited her three more times. She told Jacinta several important things: war is punishment for sin; many fashions would come that would offend Our Lord; many marriages are not of God; priests must be very pure, concentrate on their mission to the Church and souls, and be obedient to the pope and to their lawful superiors; more souls go to hell for sins of impurity than for any other; and it is important to respect priests and to do penance.

75. What happened to Lucia after the apparitions ended?

Lucia missed her cousins terribly after they died. But she knew that she was called to remain on earth for many more years; it was up to her to establish and promote devotion to the Immaculate Heart of Mary throughout the world. She remained in Fatima for some time, but after a few years the bishop decided that she should be moved elsewhere, in order to save her from the cloying, ravenous crowds. She was sent to Porto, where the Sisters of Saint Dorothy (Dorotheans) ran a girls' school.

Nobody but her mother was to know she was leaving; no one at the convent was to know her identity. Early in the morning of May 16, 1921, she was whisked away in secret. She entered the Dorothean novitiate in 1926, professed first vows in 1928, and gave final vows in 1934.

Lucia continued to receive apparitions of Our Lady and Our Lord from time to time for many years. On December 10, 1925, while she was a postulant with the Dorotheans in Pontevedra, Spain, she received the first of three apparitions, seeing Our Lady and the Child Jesus. Our Lady asked for the First Saturday Devotion, as it is known now; this was the "Communion of Reparation" that Our Lady had referred to in the July 13 apparition at Fatima. She promised to provide the graces necessary for salvation at the hour of death to those who confessed their sins, received Holy Communion, recited five decades of the Rosary, and meditated on the mysteries of the Rosary (see question 98) for fifteen minutes on the first Saturday of five consecutive months. This is to be done with the intention of making reparation to the Immaculate Heart for the sins that offended Our Lady.

On February 15, 1926, the Child Jesus appeared to Lucia to ask what she had done to spread the devotion. On December 17, 1927, Our Lord appeared to Lucia to give her permission to reveal the First and Second Secrets, but to continue keeping the Third confidential.

Our Lady appeared to Lucia once again on June 13, 1929, this time in the convent chapel at Tui, Spain. She appeared alongside the Holy Trinity, to fulfill a promise she made during the July 13 apparition at Fatima. She said she would return to ask for the consecration of Russia, and this is exactly what she did: "The moment has come in which God asks the Holy Father, in union with all the bishops of the world, to make the consecration of Russia, promising to save it by this means." We will discuss the consecration of Russia more in questions 77–79.

In May 1946, Lucia returned to the Cova da Iria and Aljustrel for just a few days. She was asked to certify the place of the apparitions, which she did. On March 25, 1948, she transferred to the Discalced Carmelites in Coimbra, Portugal, taking the religious name Sister Maria Lucia of the Immaculate Heart. When asked, she wrote a great deal about her life, the lives of Francisco and Jacinta, the many apparitions they experienced, and more. She attended the beatification of her cousins in Fatima on May 13, 2000. Sister Lucia died on February 13, 2005. Her cause for canonization is open.

76. In the 2020 film Fatima, *Harvey Keitel plays a "Professor Nichols" who interviews an elderly Lucia— by then a nun—about the apparitions. Who is Professor Nichols? Did he really interview Sister Lucia for a book?*

Professor Nichols is a fictional character, created for the purposes of framing the story of the events recounted in the film. He is depicted visiting Lucia, now a Carmelite nun in a cloistered community in Coimbra, Portugal, in 1989. Sister Lucia is telling the story to the professor, a religious skeptic who is interviewing her for an upcoming book. He is dubious, questioning Lucia at every turn, insisting that what she and the other children experienced must have some rational explanation. The questions he asks encourage Sister Lucia to reflect upon the role she and her cousins played in one of the greatest apparitions (or, from his point of view, silliest frauds) of all time.

RUSSIA

77. Was Russia properly consecrated to the Immaculate Heart of Mary, as Our Lady requested?

Yes, but it has been a long process, and this remains a somewhat controversial question for some. It was in 1929 that Our Lady returned to Lucia and made the request for Russia to be consecrated to her Immaculate Heart. Fifty-five years later, Saint John Paul II completed the consecration properly, a fact which Sister Lucia confirmed when she said that "heaven accepted" the consecration and she was assured of its valid completion and fulfillment.

78. When was this consecration done?

On March 25, 1984, after decades of incomplete attempts by various popes, Pope Saint John Paul II consecrated Russia to the Immaculate Heart of Mary. Several months in advance, the Holy Father sent a letter inviting all the bishops of the world to join him in the consecration, including the Orthodox bishops (several of whom did, in fact, join him). He studied the requirements a great deal, and even consulted with Sister Lucia to make sure it would be done appropriately and fulfill Our Lady's request. On March 25, in union with the bishops of the world, and with 200,000 pilgrims outside Saint Peter's Basilica, the pope knelt before the statue of Our Lady of Fatima, which had been brought from the Chapel of the Apparitions at the Cova da Iria. The consecration was very lengthy, and Sister Lucia said explicitly on multiple occasions that this consecration fulfilled the request of Our Lady.

79. What took so long?

It took fifty-five years to fulfill Our Lady's request for the consecration of Russia. There are many reasons for this.

It is unclear why Pope Pius XI (1922–1939) did not complete the consecration. He was pope when Our Lady's request was made, and it appears that he personally believed and had devotion to the apparitions of Our Lady of Fatima. He was not afraid to condemn Nazism and Communism vociferously. It seems likely that he was hesitant to act on the basis of a private revelation, which could have set a dangerous precedent.

Pius XII (1939–1958) was a profoundly Marian pope and was even called the "Pope of Fatima". Sister Lucia wrote to him, asking him to consecrate the world to the Immaculate Heart and make special mention of Russia, and to order all the bishops of the world to do so in union with him. It was her spiritual director who advised her to broaden the request to cover the whole world, thinking this would increase the likelihood that the Holy Father would do it. On October 31, 1942, Pius XII consecrated the world (with special mention of Russia, though not by name) to the Immaculate Heart of Mary. However, only the bishops of Portugal joined him in this. He repeated the consecration in a public ceremony at Saint Peter's Basilica on December 8, but again with only a handful of bishops. On July 7, 1952, in the apostolic letter *Sacro vergente anno*, he consecrated the people of Russia to the Immaculate Heart of Mary, but again, this was not done in union with the bishops.

Saint John XXIII (1958–1963) did not attempt a consecration. He had read the Third Secret, so he knew that Our Lady desired such a consecration. It is possible that his relatively brief pontificate (with its focus on the Second Vatican Council) precluded it.

Saint Paul VI (1963–1978) personally renewed Pius XII's 1942 consecration on November 21, 1964, during the Second Vatican Council, but did not take advantage of the Council to get all the bishops of the world to join him. On May 13, 1967 (the fiftieth anniversary of the first apparition), in the apostolic exhortation *Signum magnum*, he called for national, diocesan, and individual consecration to the Immaculate Heart of Mary.

Pope John Paul I (1978) only reigned for thirty-three days and did not attempt a consecration.

Saint John Paul II (1978–2005), as we have seen, successfully completed the consecration in 1984. Prior to that, on June 7, 1981, he attempted to consecrate Russia to the Immaculate Heart, but not in union with the bishops, so it was not fulfilled.

APPARITIONS IN THE CHRISTIAN TRADITION

80. Does the Church have some process for approving certain apparitions?

The process for approving an apparition and deeming it "worthy of belief" is detailed in the document *Norma Congregationis* ("Norms of the Congregation for Proceeding in Judging Alleged Apparitions and Revelations"), promulgated in 1978 by the Congregation for the Doctrine of the Faith. The local bishop of the area where the alleged apparitions took place may investigate the claims, as may the national conference of bishops or the Holy See. There are several criteria that are to be considered in such an investigation, among them the theological content of the apparition's messages (and their accuracy and adherence to Church teaching), the moral character of the purported seers, and the sort of spiritual fruits it promotes in the lives of the faithful. There also must be a reasonable ability to demonstrate factually that the apparitions did occur.

If a supposed apparition is starting to gain a large following, the competent authorities are expected to take action and investigate. *Norma Congregationis* does clarify that it is possible for Church authorities to approve the spiritual devotions that have developed around an alleged apparition, even if the apparition itself is not approved.

Typically, the bishop (or other ecclesiastical authority) enlists a team of experts, although the makeup of such a team depends greatly on the circumstances. The experts examine all facets of the claimed apparition, making a recommendation to the bishop, and the bishop investigates all of the materials himself and makes the final determination. Here, the words of Saint Paul are particularly apt: "Do not quench the Spirit, do not despise prophesying, but test everything; hold fast to what is good" (1 Thess 5:19–21).

81. Are there apparitions that are officially approved by the Church?

Yes, and there are different levels of approval. The Blessed Virgin Mary has appeared many times to many people, and in several instances the Church has gone through its processes and determined that the apparitions are worthy of belief.

There have been numerous apparitions, many specifically giving instruction or consolation to the individual seer. But over the last few hundred years, several of these apparitions have involved profound signs, messages for the whole world. Here are a few examples:

- *Guadalupe, Mexico (1531)*: Our Lady appeared to Saint Juan Diego and performed beautiful signs, including imprinting a miraculous image on Juan

Diego's tilma. Within ten years, over nine million natives were baptized, the worship of false Aztec gods was abandoned, and the practice of human sacrifice was brought to an end.

▪ *Rue du Bac, Paris, France (1830)*: Our Lady appeared to Saint Catherine Labouré, a novice of the Daughters of Charity, warning her of dangerous times that were to come in France, but giving her hope as well. The Miraculous Medal has its origins in this apparition, as Mary revealed to Saint Catherine how the medal should look and what it should say: "Oh Mary, conceived without sin, pray for us who have recourse to thee!"

▪ *Lourdes, France (1858)*: Our Lady appeared to Saint Bernadette Soubirous, a fourteen-year-old peasant girl. She asked for penance and reparation for the sake of sinners, and referred to herself as "the Immaculate Conception". Our Lady also provided a live spring, the waters of which have miraculous healing properties.

There are many more: Knock, Ireland, in 1879; Quito, Ecuador, from 1594 to 1634; Beauraing, Belgium in 1932–1933; Akita, Japan, in 1973; Kibeho, Rwanda, in 1981–1983; and others.

82. What does it mean for an apparition to have approval? Do Catholics have to believe the content of apparitions, or private visions, if they are approved by the Church?

If an apparition is approved by ecclesiastical authorities, it is deemed to be "worthy of belief". This is a very

intentionally chosen phrase: it is *worthy* of belief, but
the faithful are not *required* to believe it. Apparitions are
considered private revelation, and private revelation
is never considered part of the deposit of faith and is
not required to be believed. However, when they have
been approved by the competent Church authority, we
can trust that they are beneficial for the faithful and can
help us grow in the virtues of faith, hope, and charity.

83. Are the apparitions at Fatima approved by the Church?

Yes. The Church had maintained an official silence
regarding the apparitions in the years that followed the
Miracle of the Sun. Word continued to spread and pop-
ular devotion began to grow, but the Church did not
take an official position on the apparitions. Then, in
May 1922—five years after the first apparition—Bishop
da Silva of Leiria (the diocese containing Fatima) issued
a pastoral letter that indicated he would set up a commission to look into the apparitions. He wanted to be
cautious, because the apparitions had such a high profile
and accepting them without proper investigation could
lead to problems. The commission was asked to empha-
size thoroughness rather than speed.

In 1930, he issued another pastoral letter, which was
read before 100,000 pilgrims at Fatima, in which he stated:

> In virtue of considerations made known, and oth-
> ers which for reasons of brevity we omit; humbly
> invoking the Divine Spirit and placing ourselves

under the protection of the most Holy Virgin, and after hearing the opinions of our Rev. Advisers in this diocese, we hereby: 1. Declare worthy of belief, the visions of the shepherd children in the Cova da Iria, parish of Fatima, in this diocese, from May 13 to October 13, 1917. 2. Permit officially the cult of Our Lady of Fatima.

Thus, the apparitions were approved for belief, and this was done with the knowledge and consent of Pope Pius XI.

84. When did the universal Church beyond Portugal begin to develop an official devotion to Fatima?

The bishop of Leiria, with Pope Pius XI, approved the Fatima apparitions in 1930. In 1940, Pope Pius XII wrote his encyclical letter *Saeculo exeunte octavo*, on the missionary activity of the Church in Portugal, making reference to Our Lady of Fatima. The same year, Pius XII erected a new diocese in Mozambique and named Our Lady of Fatima its patroness. We can see that already the devotion to Our Lady of Fatima had moved beyond the Iberian Peninsula. Then in 1946, Pius sent a representative to Fatima to crown Mary as Queen of the World in front of 600,000 pilgrims. Pius XII would become known as the Pope of Fatima. His episcopal consecration had taken place on May 13, 1917 (date of the first apparition), and he was buried in the crypt of Saint Peter's on October 13, 1958, the anniversary of the final apparition. The feast of

Our Lady of Fatima was added to the Church's universal calendar in 2002.

There are many examples of each successive pope's devotion to Our Lady of Fatima, as we will see below in question 87.

85. If an apparition has not been officially deemed worthy of belief, am I still free to believe it?

Yes. If an official judgment has not been made in regards to a given private revelation, the Church has not taken a stance on it, and thus the faithful are free to believe, although they should certainly practice prudence, examine the contents of the revelation carefully, and proceed accordingly.

THE POPES AND
OUR LADY OF FATIMA

*86. Have popes visited the Cova da Iria and
the basilica that now stands there?*

Yes, several popes have visited the Cova da Iria—and
even more visited before becoming pope. The children
loved the pope, and Jacinta in particular prayed for him
a great deal and offered great sacrifices and suffering for
his sake. A number of popes have come and prayed
to Jacinta, including at the beatification and canonization of her and her brother.

87. What have the popes said about Fatima?

The apparitions of Our Lady of Fatima have become so
ingrained in the fabric of Catholic culture that it might
be hard to imagine a time when that was not the case.
Ever since the apparitions took place, even the popes
have been intimately involved with them.

Pope Benedict XV: He was pope at the time of the
apparitions. As we discussed in question 7, he asked
Catholics all over the world to pray a novena to Mary,
Queen of Peace, on May 5, 1917. On that same date,

he added a new intercession to the Litany of Loreto: "Queen of Peace, pray for us." Eight days later, Mary appeared for the first time to the children. We do not have a record of his having said much about the apparitions, except in a letter to the Portuguese bishops on April 29, 1918, in which he called Fatima "an extraordinary aid from the Mother of God".

Pope Pius XI: On December 6, 1929, he blessed a statue of Our Lady of Fatima to give to the Portuguese Pontifical College of Rome. Then, on October 1, 1930, he granted a partial indulgence to pilgrims traveling to Fatima. Both of these events were *before* the bishop of Leiria declared the apparitions to be worthy of belief—which, reportedly, he did with the knowledge and consent of the Holy Father.

Pope Pius XII: He has often been called the Pope of Fatima. His episcopal consecration (at the hands of Benedict XV) took place on May 13, 1917, the day of the first of Our Lady's apparitions. He once famously said, "The time for doubting Fatima has passed; the time for action is now." Pius XII spoke a great deal about Fatima, and in 1940 he entrusted a new diocese in Mozambique to the patronage of Our Lady of Fatima. On October 31, 1942, Pius consecrated the world to the Immaculate Heart of Mary; in 1946, he sent a representative to Fatima to crown Our Lady as Queen of the World, before 600,000 pilgrims. Pius is said to have personally experienced the Miracle of the Sun repeated in Rome on four separate occasions, including the day that he solemnly defined the dogma of the Assumption. On July 7, 1952, the Holy Father consecrated Russia and her people to the Immaculate Heart of Mary, in a private ceremony. This is just a sampling of Pius' actions and words on Fatima. He was buried in Saint Peter's Basilica on October 13, 1958, the anniversary of the final apparition and the Miracle of the Sun.

Pope Saint John XXIII: While he did not visit Fatima or speak publicly on it during his relatively brief papacy, Saint John XXIII (then Angelo Cardinal Roncalli) visited Fatima while patriarch of Venice on May 13, 1956.

Pope Saint Paul VI: During the closing ceremonies of the third session of the Second Vatican Council in 1964, Pope Saint Paul VI renewed Pius XII's consecration of the world to the Immaculate Heart. On May 13, 1967, Pope Saint Paul VI visited Fatima to mark the fiftieth anniversary of the apparitions and the twenty-fifth anniversary of Pius XII's consecration of the world to the Immaculate Heart of Mary. He came as a pilgrim at the invitation of the Portuguese bishops and had the opportunity to meet personally with Sister Lucia.

Pope John Paul I: John Paul I's very brief, thirty-three-day papacy did not leave much room for pronouncements on the Fatima apparitions; however, about a year before his election, on June 10, 1977, Albino Cardinal Luciani, the patriarch of Venice, led a pilgrimage of about fifty people to Fatima, during which he met with Sister Lucia.

Pope Saint John Paul II: After Pius XII, Saint John Paul II is probably the pope with the most profound connection to the Fatima apparitions. On May 13, 1981, an attempt was made on his life, and he credited his survival to the intercession of Our Lady of Fatima. He made three visits to Fatima, in 1982, 1991, and 2000. In 1984, he gifted the shrine at Fatima the bullet that came from his abdomen, which was put into the crown on the statue. During his visit on May 13, 2000, he beatified Jacinta and Francisco; he insisted on making the trip personally, in spite of his extremely fragile health. The Holy Father's profound love for Our Lady of Fatima was evident throughout his life.

Pope Benedict XVI: While he was still a cardinal, Joseph Ratzinger visited Fatima in May 2000, in preparation for Pope John Paul II's visit and the beatification. Cardinal Ratzinger was prefect of the Congregation for the Doctrine of the Faith, and as such, his responsibilities included the handling of and theological interpretation of the Third Secret of Fatima. In May 2010, a few years after his election as pope, Benedict XVI visited Fatima, said Mass, and spoke.

Pope Francis: He has also said a great deal about Fatima in his relatively few years as pontiff, but the most consequential was on May 13, 2017—the centennial anniversary of the first apparition—when he traveled to Fatima to canonize Francisco and Jacinta as saints.

88. Did Jacinta have a particular devotion to the pope?

Jacinta had a very special love for the Holy Father. She prayed for him often and offered her sufferings and sacrifices for his sake. In addition to the vision of the "bishop dressed in white" during the July 13 apparition, she had two visions involving the Holy Father.

In one, she saw him in a big house, kneeling with his head in his hands and weeping; many people were outside the house, throwing stones, cursing at him. In another vision, she saw the Holy Father praying in a church before an image of the Immaculate Heart of Mary, with many others, for those who were hungry with nothing to eat.

Her devotion to the pope did not go unacknowledged. Pope Saint John Paul II, during the Mass for the beatification of Jacinta and Francisco, explicitly thanked her for "the sacrifices and prayers she offered for the Holy Father".

CANONIZING THE VISIONARIES

89. Have the visionaries been declared saints?

Francisco and Jacinta were beatified together on May 13, 2000, by Pope Saint John Paul II. On May 13, 2017, they were canonized by Pope Francis. The cause for canonization for Sister Lucia is open and in process, but at this time she has not yet been beatified.

90. How did the process of beatification and canonization for Francisco and Jacinta play out?

Even while the visionaries were alive, they had a profound reputation for holiness. When Francisco and Jacinta both died at such young ages—and so soon after the apparitions ended—they were revered as saintly by many around the world. Over the coming years, as word of the apparitions spread further, and they became more broadly accepted and appreciated, the cult of reverence for the saintly children grew.

The official investigation into the lives of Francisco and Jacinta for the cause of their beatification began on April 30, 1952, at the diocese of Leiria. This process includes gathering all the information possible on the subjects, interviewing people who knew them closely, digging deeply into every aspect of their lives. On June 2, 1979, the documentation was sent to Rome, concluding the diocesan phase of the process.

This took longer than the process typically takes, and a big part of the delay was one rather thorny question: Can children so young be canonized? The question of the "age of reason" is at the heart of the matter here. The age of reason is the age at which a child becomes capable of understanding moral concepts to the point of being held morally responsible for his or her actions. Since the first step on the road to sainthood is for the pope to declare that the individual led a life of "heroic virtue", the question must be asked: Can children so young understand morality and the complexities of life in order to lead a life of *virtue*, to a heroic degree, so close to the age of reason?

This question was resolved in part because the Congregation for the Causes of Saints (the Vatican department that processes and investigates such matters) received a tremendous number of letters from bishops across the world arguing for the heroic virtue of the Marto children. There were 264 letters from cardinals, archbishops, bishops, nuncios, and others, many of whom were highly regarded for their theological acuity.

The saints are presented to us as models of Christian virtue and of how to live as disciples of Jesus Christ. Children need such models just as much as anyone else. This is another reason it was seen as prudent and important to continue investigating the lives of Francisco and Jacinta.

On May 13, 1989—the seventy-second anniversary of the first apparition of Our Lady—Saint John Paul II issued the decree stating that Francisco and Jacinta had lived lives of heroic virtue. Eleven years later, on May 13, 2000, after a healing due to their intercession was investigated and accepted as miraculous, he beatified them at a Mass in the Cova da Iria. After a second miracle was approved, Pope Francis canonized them on May 13, 2017, making Jacinta the youngest non-martyr ever canonized.

91. Were Francisco and Jacinta canonized because they witnessed an apparition of Mary?

Not at all. Simply witnessing an apparition, or experiencing some other private revelation, is not sufficient for canonization by the Church. While such a vision may be a mark of personal holiness, oftentimes apparitions are *calls* to holiness for someone who is patently unholy (consider Saul on the road to Damascus). Rather, the Marto children are saints because they lived lives of heroic virtue, two models of Christian discipleship, steadfastness, and fidelity to their faith in the face of suffering, persecution, threats of death, and more.

THE ASSASSINATION ATTEMPT
ON JOHN PAUL II

92. What happened on May 13, 1981?

On May 13, 1981, Pope Saint John Paul II was in Saint Peter's Square for his weekly general audience, held every Wednesday. There was a crowd of 20,000 in the square, and the pope was riding around in his car, greeting the pilgrims.

Suddenly, four shots rang out. A Turkish assassin named Mehmet Ali Ağca had shot the pope at close range, striking him with all four bullets; two of them lodged in his lower intestine, one struck his left index finger, the other his right arm. Suffering severe blood loss, the pope was rushed over to an ambulance, which had never before been used and which the Holy Father had blessed just a day prior. He was rushed to the hospital, saying along the way, "Mary, my mother! Mary, my mother!"

Ağca, the attempted assassin, was caught immediately, apprehended by the Vatican security chief, a nun, and several other spectators, who prevented him from firing more shots or fleeing.

The pope was hospitalized and nearly died, but his life was spared. He asked people to pray for Ağca, whom he had forgiven. He even met with Ağca in prison, forgiving him personally. It remains unclear why Ağca attempted to kill the pope, as he has given conflicting reasons over the years. He was sentenced to life in prison by an Italian court, but at the pope's request he was pardoned in June 2000 and deported to Turkey.

93. Why did Saint John Paul II credit Our Lady of Fatima with saving his life?

John Paul believed firmly that Mary, as Our Lady of Fatima, physically changed the trajectory of the bullets and saved his life. He came very close to dying. Because the assassination attempt took place on the anniversary of the first apparition of Our Lady of Fatima, he saw the hand of providence in the saving of his life.

94. Was this assassination attempt part of the prophecy the children received in the Third Secret? Was John Paul II the "bishop dressed in white"?

John Paul II asked for the Third Secret while he was recovering in the hospital; he was not the first pope to have read it, but as it remained secret, he had to ask to have it brought to him. As he lay in the hospital, he saw himself in the bishop dressed in white. While the bishop in the vision was killed, John Paul survived. This is part of why he saw Our Lady's hand in the events, saving him from the fate of the bishop in the vision.

CHRISTIAN DEVOTION
TO MARY

95. Why do Catholics place such importance on Mary?

It is difficult to say concisely why Catholics hold Mary in such high esteem, because there are so many reasons and facets to this. A few brief points can be made:

- Mary was the first Christian disciple. When the angel appeared to her and told her that God wanted her to be the mother of his son, she believed and gave the full assent of her will to the life and work of Jesus (cf. Lk 1:31–38).
- Jesus himself held Mary in incredibly high regard. One place this can be seen is the wedding at Cana in John's Gospel. Even though it was not yet his time, Our Lord performed a miracle at the behest of his mother (cf. Jn 2:1–11).
- She is the mother of Jesus, the Mother of God. She was a creature who bore her Creator. She is truly the Mother of God, not merely a shell containing God or some shadow of God. She is the *theotokos*, the God-bearer.
- While on the cross, Jesus gave Mary to the disciple John as his mother—which the Church has always

interpreted as a gift of Mary as mother of all Christians and of the whole Church. We are thus called in a special way to follow Jesus' example in honoring his mother.

There are many more reasons Catholics hold Mary in such high regard.

96. Do Catholics worship Mary?

No. Worship is due only to God, and Mary is not God. However, Catholics have an extraordinary respect for Mary, the Mother of God.

The difference here lies in the distinction between worship and veneration. We worship God. We venerate Mary, we admire her, we revere her. We look up to Mary as the supreme example of a Christian disciple, with unwavering faith in Jesus Christ, unflinching dedication to and acceptance of the will of God. When Jesus hung on the cross, nearing death, he gave Mary to John as his mother, and John to Mary as her son (cf. Jn 19:25–27). In doing so, Jesus gave Mary to the whole Church as mother.

Mary's purpose is to lead people to her son. Even in her requests of the children, she does not want them to make reparation for those who have offended *her;* she wants them to make sacrifice for the conversion of sinners, to bring them to her son, Jesus Christ, and to make reparation for the sins that have offended him. In her constant admonition to pray the Rosary, we see her driving people toward Christ: the Rosary is a prayerful meditation on the earthly life of Our Lord, and Mary wants nothing more than to get her children on earth to have a closer relationship with Jesus.

97. The Bible says that Jesus is the one mediator between God and man (cf. 1 Tim 2:5). So doesn't this mean that praying to Mary, or speaking to her through visions, puts her in Jesus' rightful place?

Jesus certainly is the one mediator who can reconcile us to the Father. But this does not mean that no one else can intercede for us. To make a very simple analogy: If you want your father to let you have a piece of candy, your mother might be the only mediator who can intercede on your behalf and really be effective, in a way no one else can. But this does not exclude your sister, or your grandpa, or anyone else from asking your father to give you the piece of candy. There is no contradiction here: Mary, as our mother, wants to reconcile us to her son, so she brings us to him and prays for us sinners.

Christ does not need anyone else to pray and intercede for us. He is more than capable of handling it himself. But he is pleased by our participation in his mediation. It is an act of Christian charity to pray for the good of others, and Mary desires to pray for and take care of her children.

Mary plays a significant role in God's plan of salvation, and she is a tremendously important intercessor for us here on earth. She is in continuous conflict with

Satan; he strikes at her heel, and she strikes (cf. Gen 3:15). She has appeared to so many give strength and encouragement, to give gu. how to live a Christian life, or to tell us how ν ωιε to follow God's will. We are her children (cf. Jn 19:26–27), and she appears in order to give us guidance and consolation.

98. Our Lady repeatedly told the children how important it was to pray the Rosary, and even identified herself as "the Lady of the Rosary". What is the Rosary, and how did it come about?

The Rosary is a method of meditative prayer, structured around reflecting on certain events in the life of Jesus Christ.

Mary, the Mother of God, wants nothing more than to lead people to her son. In the Rosary, we pray dozens of Hail Marys while meditating on the mysteries of Our Lord's life. The Hail Mary is an ancient Christian prayer based on phrases from the New Testament and the early Church Fathers: "Hail Mary, full of grace, the Lord is with thee. Blessed art thou among women, and blessed is the fruit of thy womb, Jesus. Holy Mary, Mother of God, pray for us sinners now and at the hour of our death. Amen."

It is not exactly clear where the Rosary came from. The use of beads to count prayers is a practice dating back to pre-Christian times; during the Middle Ages, strings of beads called "paternosters" (the Latin for

"Our Father") were used to count Our Fathers and Hail Marys. There is a tradition that Saint Dominic developed the Rosary in its current form, after a vision of Our Lady. The reliability of this tradition is questionable, but nevertheless, Saint Dominic did greatly help to spread the use of the Rosary, particularly its use in battling the Albigensian heresy. The Dominican order to this day retains a particular devotion to the Rosary.

In 1569, Pope Saint Pius V gave official approval to what we now recognize as the standard format of the Rosary: fifteen mysteries (five Joyful, five Sorrowful, five Glorious), with each mystery lasting the space of one Our Father, ten Hail Marys, and one Glory Be (another ancient prayer), or one "decade". While reciting a decade, the person praying keeps in mind one particular event in the life of Christ or of the Church, such as the Nativity, the Crucifixion, or the descent of the Holy Spirit. In 2002, Pope Saint John Paul II added the five Luminous Mysteries, which focus on the earthly ministry of Jesus.

99. Mary told the children about her "Immaculate Heart". Why does she want the world devoted to her Immaculate Heart?

Mary's Immaculate Heart is one of profound and utter love for God, for her son, Jesus Christ. It is a heart of sorrows, pierced by the wounds of Jesus, in ways only a mother's heart can be. It is a heart overflowing with love for her children, given to her by Christ on the cross. Devotion to, and veneration of, the Immaculate Heart of Mary is a way to a life of love for God, a life of Christian virtue and submission to God's will, and a life full of selfless acts of charity. This is why she, with Jesus, wants the world devoted to her Immaculate Heart; this is why she wanted Russia to be consecrated to her Immaculate Heart.

100. Was there devotion to the Immaculate Heart of Mary prior to the Fatima apparitions?

The heart of Mary has been an object of devotion throughout the history of the Church. In the Middle Ages, Saint Anselm of Canterbury and Saint Bernard of Clairvaux were some of the more prominent devotees of the heart of Our Lady. Saint Bernardine of Siena and Saint Francis de Sales also wrote about Mary's heart perfectly showing us how to love God and be devoted to Jesus Christ. Saint John Eudes was the most prominent popularizer of personal devotion to the heart of Mary, even encouraging a liturgical feast in its honor.

In 1805, Pope Pius VII for the first time instituted a feast in honor of the Immaculate Heart of Mary. In 1830, Saint Catherine Labouré introduced the Miraculous Medal, given to her during an apparition of Our Lady, which depicts the Immaculate Heart of Mary, among other images.

BIBLIOGRAPHY

Apostoli, Andrew, C.F.R. *Fatima for Today: The Urgent Marian Message of Hope.* San Francisco: Ignatius Press, 2010.

Carmel of Coimbra. *A Pathway under the Gaze of Mary: Biography of Sister Maria Lucia of Jesus and the Immaculate Heart.* 2nd ed. Washington, N.J.: World Apostolate of Fatima, 2015.

Congregation for the Doctrine of the Faith. *The Message of Fatima.* June 26, 2000.

Delaney, John J., ed. *A Woman Clothed with the Sun: Eight Great Apparitions of Our Lady.* New York: Image, 1960.

Glynn, Paul. *Healing Fire of Christ: Reflections on Modern Miracles—Knock, Lourdes, Fatima.* San Francisco: Ignatius Press, 1999.

Górny, Grzegorz, and Janusz Rosikon. *Fatima Mysteries: Mary's Message to the Modern Age.* San Francisco: Ignatius Press, 2017.

Hahn, Scott. *Hail, Holy Queen: The Mother of God in the Word of God.* New York: Doubleday, 2001.

Pitre, Brant. *Jesus and the Jewish Roots of Mary: Unveiling the Mother of the Messiah.* New York: Image, 2018.

ACKNOWLEDGMENTS

While it may go without saying that a book like this is the work of many hands, I would like to call out explicitly a few folks who made the burden light:

Mark Brumley and Tony Ryan at Ignatius Press, who thought of me and trusted me to start and complete this project in such an incredibly short time, and who provided me an opportunity to write on Our Lady, whom I love so much;

The Ignatius Press production team, whose eagle-eyed editing turned a rough manuscript into something presentable;

Father Andrew Apostoli (1942–2017), C.F.R., whose tremendous research on the Fatima apparitions served as an inspiration and important source for the present work;

Dr. Edward Sri, for providing a foreword to the book, and for his informative scholarship on the Blessed Virgin Mary;

Saints Francisco and Jacinta, and Sister Lucia, to whom I prayed every night, asking for their intercession;

And, of course, my dear wife and children, whose patience during the writing of this book has been unsurpassed. Without their support, and that of my wider family, I truly would not have been able to do this.

chanel
83 Good
get TV
Bed